RIT - WALLACE LIBRARY
CIRCULATING LIBRARY BOOKS

OVERDUE FINES AND FEES FOR <u>ALL</u> BORROWERS

*Recalled = $1/ day overdue (no grace period)
*Billed = $10.00/ item when returned **4** or more weeks overdue
*Lost Items = replacement cost+$10 fee
*All materials must be returned or renewed by the duedate.

SEVEN POWERFUL STRATEGIES
TO ACCELERATE YOUR BUSINESS

If you are leading a small to midsize business, you know the drill. Compared to the behemoths roaming the global markets, you have limited resources, shallower pockets, fewer in-house MBAs, and more at risk. You understand what "lonely at the top" means.

Beneath the Armor identifies seven strategies defined by your most successful peers to provide you with a roadmap to overcome your isolation and scarcity of assets.

The strategies are simple, relevant, and within your capabilities to implement. Attempting to apply the doctrines and strategies of the big business tycoons has frustrated you. Finally, you have a book that is dedicated to addressing your specific needs.

BENEATH THE ARMOR

BENEATH THE ARMOR

How Leaders of Small to Midsize Businesses

Stand Tall in a Turbulent Global Economy

OLE CARLSON

To order additional copies of this book, contact:
Xlibris Corporation
1-888-795-4274
www.Xlibris.com
Orders@Xlibris.com
22366

Contents

Dedication

Beneath the Armor is dedicated to the TEC Tribe. For those of you outside the circle, let me make an introduction. The TEC International Tribe consists of past and present board of directors, owners, leaders, staff, CEO, KEY, and TEC associate members, speakers, internal and external trainers, and anyone else who has been personally touched by this extraordinary organization over the past 50 years.

Above all, this book is dedicated to my love, Sue Ann, who has entered my life to teach me who I am, to engage me in unconditional love, and to play with me like I have never played before.

Acknowledgments

"Beneath the flimflam of the Christmas letter
lurks the heart of a legitimate writer."

—Al Libke

Al is a fraternity brother, friend, and physician. Those words were scribbled on the back of a returned Christmas letter that I had mailed to friends and family in the late 1960s. The message has haunted me for decades. Al, I am sorry it took almost 35 years, but here it is.

One more person, among scores of others, needs to be acknowledged. Jim Jensen, entrepreneur, CEO, and mentor, entered my life at a time when I was wandering and offered me an opportunity and vision of myself that seemed out of reach. It was not. I shall always be grateful. Jim started me on my journey of exploration, success, and doing what I was meant to do and being who I was meant to be.

Introduction

Getting an idea should be like sitting on a pin.
It should make you jump up and do something.

—E. L. Simpson

In a recent network television commercial, two buttoned-down pinstripe business consultants are sitting across the desk from an interested and attentive CEO. A comprehensive and apparently costly new re-engineering approach for the CEO's business is being proposed and thoughtfully considered. When the recommendation is concluded, the CEO nods favorably toward them and says, "This looks fantastic. When do you get started?"

The two consultants quickly exchange astonished glances. One of the experts, eyebrows arching and failing to conceal an emerging smirk, replies to the CEO, "We don't actually *do* what we propose." Dead silence. The scene concludes with the consultants walking through the building's lobby, embossed leather briefcases swinging, heads shaking side to side with one softly muttering to the other, "I can't believe he actually expected us to *do* the work."

If you are the leader of a small to midsize business, this is all-too-familiar territory. Consultants, board members, professional service providers, and a vast assortment of others outside the walls of your organization are willing to volunteer suggestions on how you should run your business. When the lights are turned off and everyone except you has gone to the comforts of home, it all comes to a sobering halt. You are left with the doing. It is your time, your money, your energy, and your expertise that you draw upon while the advisors circle the perimeter and critically gaze through the windows. You have not corralled a herd of MBAs down the hall to launch state-of-the-art strategies like Jack Welch did and could. You know at a subatomic particle level what "lonely at the top" implies. Welcome to the intersection where the buck either stops or is passed on.

What do you do? Read and constantly refer to *Beneath the Armor*. Deliberately tap into the triumphant real-life, real-time, and real-money knowledge of honorable leaders pulling oars similar to yours. Learn what other cream-of-the-crop leaders have done to get to the next level of their business and accelerate skyward on their bell-shaped curve. Most of you have been at the helm of your businesses with a high-courage, low-to-medium competency model. It was what you had to do to get to where you are. I cannot boost the courage quotient. That is all about your DNA. What I can increase is your competency (if you're willing).

By purchasing this book, I assume you want to be more successful doing what you do. I know you are frustrated reading the volumes of best-selling business books authored by the giants of American business when you do not have the resources they possess. I imagine you are embarrassed and indignant about being associated with the high-profile, get rich-by-any-means business leaders who crowd today's police beat headlines. Can you honestly relate to what the tycoons are doing relative to your business? Are you tired of faddish, philosophical, and ever-changing academic approaches to leading a successful enterprise? Do you hunger for a resource that is relevant, congruent and calibrates with what you are dealing with day to day? If I am on target and hitting an exposed nerve, keep reading.

Beneath the Armor springs from multiple wells. For 17 years, I have had an association with The Executive Committee (TEC) International, a San Diego-based global forum for owners, CEOs, presidents, and executives of small to midsize businesses. TEC International's mission is to increase the effectiveness and enhance the lives of business leaders.

Through the TEC model, I have spent in excess of 15,000 hours facilitating CEO group meetings, teaching strategy workshops, and participating in one-on-one coaching sessions with thousands of successful corporate leaders from all types of businesses representing multiple industries. I played the role of advocate, teacher, facilitator, challenger, conscience, consultant, friend, counselor, and occasionally a pain in the butt. These meetings, workshops, and conversations took place month after month, year after year, enabling me to witness firsthand what business leaders confronted, what was considered, what was implemented, and what actually worked. It was real life, in real time, risking and spending real money, with real get-your-attention consequences. It was, as Dr. Phil would say, the real deal.

I stood shoulder to shoulder with executives witnessing the agony of executing a layoff, firing an under-performing employee, making payroll with credit cards, or sheepishly borrowing, once again, from in-laws. I was present watching leaders stumble into the office, exhausted after sleeping on a hard pillow all night worrying about losing a key customer, having a note immediately due, or facing a difficult, gut-wrenching conversation. I celebrated with my clients when they triumphed over impending competitors or handed out sizeable bonus checks. I deeply understood their pride when ushering a company tour, showing prospective customers what they had created, and what they could offer. I was present, entrenched on the front line when it was happening. I was in the foxhole, armed and dangerous, learning what worked.

My TEC members and I had the opportunity to participate in monthly three-hour business seminars conducted by experts current on every imaginable business and personal growth topic. Curriculum from these workshops filled my professional and private toolbox with fresh perspectives and potent actions to explore with customers and with myself. I had my own live, in the moment, business and personal growth laboratory, testing processes, strategies, and tactics while measuring results.

I have conducted more than 450 interactive strategic business seminars with CEO audiences in the United States, United Kingdom, Canada, Mexico, and Australia. The agendas dealt with innovative leadership ideas and proven best practices. Corporate clients, TEC members, and I gained enormously by experiencing and applying what I learned from these workshops to businesses that I influenced.

Beneath the Armor reveals seven potent, irrefutable business strategies to accelerate your business forward and upward. The strategies originate from business leaders who have been there and done that. Forget giving them a t-shirt, they deserve Armani. Their fingerprints, footprints, and dental records are all over the following chapters. You do not need to invent anything. You do not need to think and act out of the box. Implement in your own individual style. Do not assume that you know these strategies or are currently executing them. I did the heavy lifting and sorting. I isolated and simplified the significant seven because they are valid, relevant, and calibrate with you and your business.

Be careful to not discount the first blush simplicity of what is being suggested in this book. In my experience working with business leaders, there is a desire on your part to discover and believe that there is a "silver bullet" to finally and ultimately be told the "exact truth" about how to succeed in business. The Lone Ranger was the only one who had silver bullets that affected the people he encountered. Forget that notion. Sorry, it is not going to work! Too many of you are more than willing and much too eager to place your faith in and subordinate your experience to "expert advice."

Authors and consultants are anxious to suggest that they and only they have the "magic sauce" that provides the ultimate ingredients to your success. You have been subjected to *Total Quality Management, Re-engineering, Open Book Management, Quality Circles, Empowerment, Excellence and Award Programs, 360 Degree Feedback Encounters, Top Down, Bottom Up, Learning Organizations*, and countless other state-of-the-art business disciplines designed to shape and sharpen your business. It is overwhelming and ultimately much too confusing. Let these business flavors of the month flow by like a bubbling brook, and once in awhile, when a piece of the offering appears to fit your business, dip your net into the passing stream and fish out that element of the program that works for you. There is no "one ultimate way" to be successful.

You can rely on my research and experience with thousands of victorious leaders and my ability to pass on to you what really works and what does not. I am the conduit and the channel to your peers who have defined the pathway to being successful. Be mindful that in the past you have only had you and your immediate inner circle. That is your limitation and perhaps a potentially foul-smelling albatross hanging around your neck. I am exposing you to thousands of success stories showing you "a" path. I am your personal valet helping you to suit up, arming you with the seven strategies, and preparing you for your next joust in this global business environment. Begin immediately. No need to wait, but please not all at once. Be patient *(I know that's not in your DNA)*. Keep in mind you have done fine up to this juncture but here is a little help.

Beneath the Armor will inspire you to:

- Come out from behind your corporate mask and be truly authentic.
- Take better care of yourself in order to more effectively lead others.
- Identify and adhere to enduring principles in your enterprise.
- Lead the organization by growing your human currency.
- Remain steadfast as the market swirls about and accelerates.
- Be accountable for how you influence the people in your organization.
- Upgrade the talent in your organization.
- Understand the importance of being financially healthy.
- Remain flexible and responsive to changing business environments.
- Focus on what the organization is willing to provide to the market.

This book is not a passive reading experience with you lounging in front of a crackling fire, sipping an exalted 2000 vintage Bordeaux, although that is neither a bad picture nor a faulty idea. You have some cooking to do. People are going to show up shortly and they are hungry for your leadership. The learning is generative and consumptive, rich and plentiful. Grab your hi-liter and laptop. Approach this information as if it really mattered. It does. It ought to. This plate is where the majority of your meat and potatoes lie, where your net worth resides, where you spend most of your time, what drains or jumpstarts your energy, what engages your emotions, your intellect and ultimately makes uncompromising demands on your physical, emotional, and psychological well-being. You and I are members of the elite and informed tribe who really get this.

Each chapter concludes with you participating in exercises and journal work anchoring the strategies and propelling you forward, upward, and hopefully, beyond where you currently reside. Demand deliberate and intentional action from yourself rather than settling for an intellectual cocktail party understanding of the material.

There are new frontiers for you to explore, markets to penetrate and a business that deserves your absolute utmost attention to meet the needs and demands of your employees, customers, family, and most importantly, yourself.

I insist that your personal and professional life be easier, more prosperous, more joyful, more fulfilling, and more in balance. It is important that you value yourself as much as I value you. I am your most devoted and attentive advocate. I want you to sweep a staggering stack of chips off the table when you have arrived at your knowing when to hold 'em and when to fold 'em crossroads. Understanding and implementing these strategies will speed you to where you desire and deserve to go.

You have arrived at an important intersection of your professional and personal life. By reading *Beneath the Armor*, you have demonstrated a commitment to become better at what you do. You have dedicated yourself to be more successful, to reach your full potential, to not settle and to be more accountable. You have decided to up the ante, raise the bar, and exceed previous expectations.

Congratulations! Now, get busy. Cling to what works for you. Ride it for all it is worth. Discard what has become habitual, comfortable, or familiar but no longer serves you and the organization well. It is a brand-new day that is going to be much different from yesterday and tomorrow much different from today. The velocity of change and world competition is accelerating. There are predators outside your company door capturing your market share, pursuing your clients, and seducing your key employees.

Wear your suit of armor well, and execute the seven strategies as you stride out into today's business environment. I wish you good fortune. Stand tall!

Chapter One

STRATEGY ONE: BE AUTHENTIC, IT'S EASIER TO REMEMBER

It's not easy being green.

—Kermit the Frog

**Be who you are and not who you
think you should be.**

People construct personas to create a desired impression on any given audience. At times, these contrived personalities serve us well by protecting us, getting us what we need or allowing us to pass through a difficult moment with as few emotional, psychological, and physical abrasions as possible. For many, the different characters we assume are vital and essential survival mechanisms.

Some of the roles we play are consciously and deliberately scripted. Others are unconscious or bio-reactive responses automatically launched from deeply embedded silos in our psyche. The danger lies in the roles being inappropriate or implementing strategies that no longer serve us or others well. Anonymous said, "When the horse is dead get off." It is good advice, especially if you are the leader of an organization performing in front of varied internal, external, and critical audiences.

While in college, I had a variety of looks and behaviors depending upon where I was, whom I was with, and what I was doing. I had the "party animal" look, which differed greatly from the "going to a friend's house for dinner" guise. Occasionally, I had the bewildered "deer in the headlights" exterior when I was clueless and did not know what to say or do. Perhaps in those instances I was most genuine. I have noticed that many CEOs wear a variety of masks depending upon the circumstances. It must be confusing to the people who are consistently with them in those various occasions. "Hey boss, customer, vendor, friend, spouse, parent, just who are you, really?"

Often I was an impostor; the contrived pretender unsure that what I had to offer would suffice and be accepted. The journey to authenticity and self-acceptance was long and at times terrifying. It had starts and stops. It had excitement and despair. It had acceptance and rejection. It covered the full range of the human experience. Ultimately, it was a necessary and noble passage that I highly recommend to business leaders, or anyone else out there in the world doing the best that they can to discover who they really are.

One of the early personalities was the role I fabricated as a copier salesperson for the Xerox Corporation (I'm sounding more like Sibyl with every line I write). Fresh out of college, with a liberal arts degree fluttering in my hand, I convinced the Northwest Region Xerox branch manger to turn me loose in downtown Seattle, Washington peddling copiers. I had my "confident, I can do anything" character locked in forward gear. To create my new and unfamiliar business image, I purchased four single-breasted inexpensive wool suits from a two-for-one university district college clothier, bought a synthetic leather briefcase, polished my scuffed fraternity-issue brown wingtips, and scampered out to take head-on 3M, AB Dick, and Thermo-Fax. Xerox was king. The Japanese had yet to enter the market.

On the first day, in a downtown business-district territory, I scurried past a window display at a national department store. I was in a hurry to make my first sale. Slow down! It caught my eye, a black-and-gray houndstooth hat set on top of a male mannequin outfitted in the most current and fashionable Madison Avenue professional attire. Perfect—just what I needed to complete the look of what I perceived a high-rolling professional Xerox salesperson should project. Buy it.

Briskly and confidently, I walked out of the store with my new cap perched on my head. Later, feeling utterly conspicuous, I scurried about my territory with limited success. I was doing things right but not doing the right things. I was rigid, unsure of myself attempting to be true to an image that felt intuitively distant and unrelated.

The new business bonnet got in the way. I looked like a young Paul "Bear" Bryant without a championship Southeast Conference football team to coach. Feeling utterly inadequate masquerading as an experienced copier salesperson, I flopped and floundered in trying to be the whiz-bang sales hotshot I thought I would automatically become by wearing that hat. I was memorizing, scripting, costuming, and pretending to be someone I was not. I was a rigid, predictable robot long before robotics came onto assembly lines. Label me "Robo salesman" stumbling my way through the steel and glass canyons of downtown Seattle. Veteran Xerox salespeople snickered behind my back, and customers found this attire incongruent with the person in front of them. The hat became a symbol of phoniness, and one day, it was forever banished to a basement closet, never to crown my head again.

The next four quarters, sans hat and sporting a new attitude, I reset my look and strategy. It was a "no brainer." If I had persisted on doing what I had been doing, I would be standing 10 deep in an unemployment line wearing that silly cap shuffling along with the rest of the underachievers. I took a cleansing breath, reaching far inside and let Ole out. Whoooooooooooosh. It was a scary and uneven evolution, but it eventually worked. At times, I felt and may have looked like a large inflated balloon with the air suddenly escaping, flying about in unpredictable directions, bumping into walls, and jettisoning about. Miraculously, I never ran out of air and unexpectedly led the Northwest Region for that period in total copier and supplies sales. I was the comeback poster-child salesperson of the year. My colleagues ceased their snickering after my sales manager publicly cut me a bonus check larger than anything I could have ever imagined, and more substantial than most of them had experienced in their careers. "So there!"

Hatless and bank deposit slip in hand, I discovered that the secret to my newly acclaimed business triumph was to simply be myself and forget about conforming to the mannequin in the gray flannel suit and houndstooth hat. It was not who I was. It was a life-altering lesson for a 23-year-old "rookie" who did not know much about business but was learning a great deal about himself. As Judy Garland once said, "Always be a first-rate version of yourself, instead of a second-rate version of somebody else."

Internally, I had ambition, curiosity, a diligent work ethic, and an innocent naivety. Not imitating others proved to be the path to success. What was already inside of me was sufficient and more accessible than ever-changing images to portray and scripts to recite. I learned that to be authentic and effective, I had to eliminate, not add, to be more of who I really was and less of who I thought I should be. In retrospect, it seems so obvious.

I joyfully discovered and was quite relieved that one bona fide "look" would be sufficient and usher me safely and successfully through life. All that was required was to fully show up and stay conscious. Woody Allen was right. How simple. Show up! The houndstooth and its accompanying contrived personality placed a lid on my potential and natural abilities. The Xerox hat became a sombrero to hide under and to unconsciously snooze beneath. What was essential was to be present, pay attention, and remain awake in a world that was consistently falling asleep. It just might be a competitive advantage. It was my first lesson in being authentic, being an original.

Through the years, I have witnessed numerous leaders of small to midsize businesses hide behind masks that did not particularly serve them well or represent who they really were. They were just as guilty as I was. Is that you behind there? Are you wearing the face that your father left you? Did this look come from a management book? Are you the personification of a college professor you took a class from, or are you just making it up as you go along? Take stock. Something is working in your professional career by your being who you are. Nice going. Why not all the time? You are sitting in a seat that few successfully occupy. Congratulations! You are certainly not Jack Welch. You never have been, and there is a 100 percent chance that you never will be. You are just you, and that is enough.

Bring your best self forward and change what is not working.

Let us be clear. I am not saying that "being yourself" gives you permission to be a complete authentic jerk. You know people who deliberately hide behind despicable behavior claiming that they were just being real. They were simply getting clutter off their chests, clearing the air, being candid and forthright. A leader justifying and rationalizing this kind of behavior can cause irreparable destruction to the culture and human spirits in the business. It is selfish, shameful, and cowardly. They may feel better but the wake they leave behind is an intolerable toxic tidal wave flooding the organization with damaged human currency. What they have unilaterally decided is to take a short-term gain (not controlling or being accountable for their destructive behavior) for a long-term loss (high turnover, low morale, obedient employees).

Steve was a branch manager I worked for in another industry. He lacked a formal education; however, he was acutely streetwise and knew how and when to take care of himself. Self-interest he fully understood. He had risen to an impressive position in the company by being in the right place at the right time. On occasion, proper timing and extraordinary luck does work. Steve had far exceeded his life's dreams and aspirations. He was making more money and had more authority than he ever thought possible. Life was good for Steve with a senior executive vice president title, a luxury import automobile, and a split-level suburban home bordering a lush, manicured fairway.

Steve was a bully in a silk sports coat cloaked as the leader of six already successful salespeople. We were generating sizable quarterly bonus checks for him and his family. With his gun cocked and loaded, a nervous finger on the trigger, and his salespeople in the crosshairs, Steve was ready and willing to put down anyone who threatened his newly found prosperity and status in life.

On Monday mornings, somewhere around eight o'clock, Steve conducted the weekly sales meeting. They were dreadful, self-esteem eroding occasions. The gatherings were poorly planned, unproductive, and shamefully unprofessional. Essentially, they were a platform for Steve to belittle, embarrass, threaten, and harass his sales force. Steve held forth to his obedient audience with no sustainable substance. The farther the individual or team was from making quota and reaching their goals, the more destructive and frightened Steve became. He was not concerned about our individual success, only his mattered. What frightened Steve was how our performance might negatively reflect on him and potentially threaten his position with the company and his recently celebrated lifestyle. He was wholly focused on and totally immersed in himself. We were either his escalator to further glory, or a ticket on the down elevator to his previous unsatisfactory blue-collar life.

Anything and everything was fair game for our branch manager on those appalling Monday mornings. Nothing was sacred or off limits. Nothing! He assaulted and penetrated barriers that would horrify any human resources director or corporate labor lawyer. Discussions of sexual conquests, drinking excursions, off-color jokes, and other non-business taboo topics sprinkled our Monday morning agendas.

I recall one meeting when he noticed that Dave, a recently hired salesperson, had an obvious case of halitosis. Protocol or basic decency might suggest that Steve address that situation off line. Not a chance! Not in Steve's world of sales management. He bellowed out in full volume to Dave and to the rest of us startled Certs-chomping observers that "his new salesman's breath smelled like horseshit." Welcome to Steve's rendition of professional sales leadership.

If events were not going the way he thought they should,

he would spontaneously explode; his puffy jowls suddenly expanding like a blowfish, his furrowing forehead turning various shades of scarlet, his darting eyes narrowed and penetrating; his mouth spewing out spittle-laced profanity. He shouted, pounded his stubby fist on the table, while sputtering and stumbling over a limited and crude vocabulary. Eventually, when the eruption had subsided and his sales force turned to solid lava, he would terminate the meeting demanding that everyone get back to work and close some damn sales or else. Not a pretty picture.

The dictum was too late. The tsunami had moved inland. Foundations had been washed away and solid structures uprooted. The damage had been done.

Steve felt great. He suggested that it was a "Terrific meeting. Don't you all agree?" It was all off his ample self-serving chest. He viewed himself as a straight shooter who told it like it is. Steve wanted real men on his sales team. He was not like Jack Nicholson in the movie *A Few Good Men* who believed Tom Cruise "couldn't handle the truth." He obviously thought that we could deal with anything that he put forth, but in reality, we were not behaving like real men, and we did not handle what he was putting forth. We were silently returning to our safe havens away from the office or behind closed doors in private sanctuaries where we dealt with the humiliation in our own manner. We were collectively a disservice to Steve. Nobody confronted him on his style or his behavior. No one was willing to come forward and express the negative impact that his *leadership* was having on the organization or on us. It was deemed too risky. An unseen landmine might be stepped on and ignite another explosion. We were like many business teams who played it safe, silently colluding and hoping through divine intervention that Steve would change and become the leader that we all desired and deserved. We were as cowardly as Steve.

Meanwhile, with his revenue stream gargling Listerine,

tossing life preservers, and removing emotional shrapnel, Steve blundered on. His behavior was triggered by fear and insecurity. He did not enter the world with those traits. Steve ignored his birthright authenticity, and instead, chose a conditioned and learned response that separated him from his true self. His behavior had nothing to do with a higher purpose or any noble pursuit. He operated at his lowest and most unproductive level. Slowly but constantly, he was extinguishing the flame that he so desperately wanted to protect.

Steve's inability to appropriately manage his emotions of fear, anger, and anxiety was his eventual downfall. Blowing up and letting off steam may have been cathartic to him, but the rest of us were scampering off to emergency wards. Others eventually noticed. The company was subsequently sold, and the new owner immediately dismissed him and his leadership ways.

French philosopher Pierre Teilhard de Chardin perhaps said it best: "We are not human beings having a spiritual experience, we are spiritual beings having a human experience." Unfortunately, Steve allowed his human experience to dominate and block access to his spiritual, authentic self. The leader that Steve could have been was already inside of him. He had allowed his fearful ego to hold his authentic self hostage.

From the Zen tradition comes a story about a sculptor who had chiseled an incredible, anatomically perfect statue of an elephant out of an ancient and ugly granite rock. One day an admirer asked the artist, "How did you create such a beautiful animal out of that old ugly rock?" The sculptor humbly replied, "I simply chipped away all of the stone that was not the elephant." Take it off. Take it all off! It is all inside of you and you need to let it shine.

I am not suggesting that you become a post-modern new millennium messiah walking through the plant in a white robe hugging and distributing flower petals to your employees. The "group grope" approach has shortcomings as it decelerates decision-making, involves too many people, and handcuffs leaders. I am not asking you to toss a bunch of feathered pillows around people when wanting to get something accomplished. What I am asking you to examine is: Are your actions and behaviors furthering the individual, group, or organization in a positive and constructive manner? If what you are initiating is only going to benefit yourself and paralyze your employees, then hit the reverse gear and reconsider

How will your message best be heard? You do not need to be perfect. Perfection is futile and neurotic work. Give it up. I am advocating that you be appropriate, and if what you are doing is not working, try something different. Pay attention.

Effective leaders are able through self-awareness and intention to manage, sort and select their impulses according to what they are encountering. They have the ability to delay gratification and place inappropriate responses on hold. It is the right thing to do. Your people will appreciate and respond in a positive manner to it.

Individualize and give permission for others to do the same.

Business leaders come in a variety of packages. It is Heinz 57. There is no defined formula in assembling the perfect chief. The business leader tribe is a multifaceted, differentiated, individualistic assortment of talents and characteristics. One thing I have noticed having worked with thousands of leaders of small to midsize businesses is that the blatantly successful ones are truly individualized, self-actualized human beings and are able to convey their individuality to the people that they influence, inspire, and transform.

When I walked the corridors of successful small to midsize companies, I did not find an overabundance of, "yes people." There were not many conformists strolling along side of me humming some familiar tune of corporate compliance. Missing were a multitude of phonies, impostors, and charlatans in these flourishing businesses. These executives did not have at their disposal sophisticated marketing departments creating their images and branding their identities. They were on their own, naked as the eyes of a clown, willing to stand in the organizational spotlight, warts and all. When the blemishes got in the way, they removed or censored them instead of stubbornly insisting to ignore or cover up what was producing negative outcomes.

Steve, my former branch manager, was not a part of this group. He was participating with the other folks. Granted, the winners occasionally lost their tempers, did not always do everything just right, say the right thing at the right moment, but people understood their humanity, and above all, trusted their intentions.

I had the privilege of working with Jeff. He was a member of the TEC Group that I facilitated in Seattle for 15 years. He made an attempt at college but was too impatient to go through four years of formal education before marking his score in life. Jeff dropped out of university after a couple of years. This young entrepreneur danced and sang to a different tune. At age 20, he married his high school sweetheart, took a whack at corporate America, did well, but did not fit.

With borrowed funds, exhausted savings and a friend for a partner, he started his company. At first, it was bumpy, and he and his partner spent most of their time on the road, building distribution channels, relationships, and customers. They were away from their families and familiar surroundings. It was their road much traveled.

There were occasions when payroll had to be financed with personal credit cards, payables stretched and receivables accelerated, but he stayed the course and eventually built a sizable net worth by growing the business, taking risks and investing wisely. Eventually, he was living on the lake, luxury yacht docked out front and living the good life.

Jeff was an absolute original. What you saw at work, at the country club, with his family, at church, you witnessed at home. He consistently wore the same face. How you experienced Jeff in a TEC meeting was exactly how he was in all other situations. I always knew what to expect when I was with Jeff, and so did the people who worked for him. Jeff was without fail what he claimed to be and his behavior constantly reinforced and claimed his identity. He was predictably generous, entrepreneurial, available, fun loving, shrewd, and willing to take risks. Being fired by Jeff was a ticket to a sizable severance package. If you needed a loan, he was available, financing for a new house, no problem. He took care of his family, employees, and friends without asking anything in return. He was so good and gracious to others that when he occasionally was inappropriate, it was quickly forgiven and forgotten.

One day, I was facilitating a planning session for him and his management team. I had allowed the group to slide off into an unproductive discussion regarding mission statements. They began arguing about whether or not a certain word meant this or meant that, if what they provided the customer was on purpose, mission or vision? Should the right word be "dedicated" or "committed"? Does this sound familiar?

Their leader was becoming more irritated as the conversation drifted into what he termed "silliness." In retrospect, I agree. It had and I had allowed it to happen. Shame on the facilitator! Finally, after about 20 minutes of silliness, Jeff stood up, obviously upset, and proclaimed the meeting over, finished! He ordered his management team to stop wasting his and their time. Slamming his fiscal year budget on the table, he suggested, in no uncertain terms that they immediately go out and sell something, count inventory, order supplies, call their corporate attorney or do anything instead of continuing to do what they were doing.

"Let's not let this happen again." His words were not entirely unlike the message that Steve consistently delivered. How it was delivered, received, and perceived was the difference.

Jeff had made enough positive deposits (Steve Covey-like) into his team that people could hear and respect what he was saying. They understood that he was right, that his intention was purely developmental and not punitive. Steve, on the other hand, had made so many destructive withdrawals from his sales force that the account was chronically overdrawn and the damage permanent.

Jeff demonstrated his humanness. He was not perfect but he was saying to his management team that it is O.K. to blow it once in awhile. Not all the time, but nobody is handed their walking papers for making an occasional mistake. To Jeff, mistakes are simply "mis-takes." When a "mis-take" occurs in filming a movie production, the director simply asks the actors to do it over and learn from the previous attempt. Jeff conveyed to all of us that we were not mistakes; we were simply making one.

Jeff said to his management team that it is safe to bring all of yourself into this building. You do not have to check parts of yourself at the door unless your objective is to only satisfy yourself and not the organization. Bring it on, but you had better learn! People are shown to the door for not learning. They learned and so did he.

Jeff was acknowledged as, the TEC Group's "Godfather." Members respected him and sought his advice on personal and professional matters. His status was well earned as he consistently extended himself to all members. Over the years, group members came and went, but Jeff was there month after month providing stability and continuity. He represented everything that was good and effective in this unique gathering of successful and authentic CEOs.

After 15 years, I left that group in February 2002 to satisfy my writing hunger and to expand my speaking career. It was time. During the last meeting, I conducted a ceremony where I told each of the 15 members how and what they had contributed to my life. I spoke from my heart and personalized my comments. Other hearts around the table opened as I offered my truth and experience with and about each member. When I concluded the exercise, Larry, president of a regional public bank, insisted that we reverse the process and have each member speak of my contribution to his or her lives. I half-heartedly protested. It was wonderfully rewarding as I listened to each member tell me what I had meant to them. I could have gone several more laps around that table. It was Ole's 15 minutes of fame, and I did not want it to end.

The "Godfather" was the last to share. He attempted to make eye contact but emerging and unanticipated tears blurred his vision. He struggled to speak but surging unfamiliar emotions idled his tongue and constricted his throat. Jeff slowly and deliberately nodded his head toward me, his right hand clenched in a fist, his thumb pointed skyward. Jeff remained silent but everyone at the conference table understood his message. That is not even an assumption. The communication was flawless. How is yours?

It was an unintended, authentic moment that will remain in the group memory for a lifetime. Jeff, TEC Group 192's "Godfather," his kimono wide open, revealing to his colleagues, peers, and me, who he really was and what he was feeling. He was truly present, in the moment, coming out from behind his eyes with no excuses, no apologies, and perhaps just slightly embarrassed. Jeff had everyone's attention because we understood that his intent was pristine, pure, authentic, and unanticipated. The invitation is for you to take the risk. Step out. Reveal. It is well worth the journey and others will follow. You want that, right?

Update your "story"; the old one may be obsolete.

I grew up in an absolute destitute family. Dysfunctional does not quite capture it. I understand it is relative, but the manner in which this band of characters chose to experience life was absurd and unnecessary. It was a chapter in my life, seasoned with poverty, emotional abuse, and accompanied with a hearty dose of fundamental daily survival. I was on the 50-yard line, chin in hand, witnessing in naïve wonderment, severe alcoholism, domestic emotional and physical violence, sheriff foreclosures, and bottom of the barrel self-esteem. That was the Carlson family.

When I was nine years old my 11-year-old sister and I were unexpectedly shipped off on a Greyhound bus from Bell Gardens, California to Tacoma, Washington to live with a variety of then distant relatives. Timetables were a bit vague. That schedule may have troubled others, but to us it seemed normal. Mysteriously, our parents remained huddled in a slum trailer park in East Los Angeles plotting their next move to escape the bill collectors, encroaching neighborhood crime, and a worsening degradation of their lives.

Somewhere between Fresno and Mt. Shasta, without seeking counsel from my self-appointed savior sibling, I decided that the Carlsons were untrustworthy, and if anyone was going to take care of Ole, it was going to be me. It was a heady and intoxicating decree to make for an innocent young boy not yet a decade on the planet. I concluded that independence and autonomy would be the strategies that would best serve me from this juncture on. Those words were not a part of my childhood vocabulary, but I clearly understood the concepts and felt comfortable with my decision.

Behind an ivory-colored steering wheel, periodically slumped beneath a "Don't talk to the driver" public notice, veteran Greyhound bus driver, Mike, obediently and boringly steered our vehicle north. Unbeknownst to him, in a window seat way in the back row of his musty and nearly empty bus, a story was being formed that would be my north star for years to come. We never know when we are participating in someone's transformation, do we?

As the Interstate 5 countryside passed by the dirty sliding-glass bus window, I claimed accountability for creating my future. Subsequently, through the years, I earned my own money, chose my friends, lived where I wanted to live, went to schools that I selected, and did exactly what I wanted to do. Nobody could tell this loner anything. Concepts of negotiation, intimacy, connection, community, feedback, family, and sharing were not on the radar screen. I was a great team player as long as I led the team. "Now everybody, huddle up and do it my way."

The strategy appeared to work as I broke free from the tyranny of the Carlson clan and created a life for myself that far exceeded anything that my immediate family had ever experienced or envisioned for me. Evidence suggested that I was riding the right rail. I became the only person in my immediate family to finish high school. I was awarded an academic/athletic scholarship to attend and eventually graduate from the University of Washington. I was employed by *Fortune 500* companies and earning a six-figure income. I became a member of prestigious country clubs, socialized with professionals, and lived in exclusive high-income residential neighborhoods. It was not always a straight-line ascent; I had my temporary setbacks. Fellow bus companion, sister Judy, met the income and position benchmark later on in her life but that is another story. She should tell it to you. She is an inspiration.

Unanticipated, the autonomous story surprisingly had

numerous latent liabilities. I invited a psychologist to speak to my TEC Group and conduct a personality profile on each member. I participated and was tested along with the rest of the group. After completing and submitting the questionnaire, the psychologist later telephoned with the results. I was congratulated for being number one. I asked, "In what category?" He replied, "Having tested over 10,000 people, you scored number one in autonomy." I asked, "Is that a good thing or a bad thing?" He responded, "It depends. How is it currently working?" I hate questions like that.

Two marriages later and with a reputation of being arrogant, aloof, and a lone wolf, I questioned whether my story was still effective. Evidence was clearly indicating that what once served me well was currently floundering on the rocks and about to break apart. A former wife once asked if she could make me a sandwich and I said, "No thanks, I wasn't hungry." Five minutes later, I made a tuna fish sandwich on whole wheat for myself, absolutely astounded and bewildered that she would subsequently make that incident a topic of concern and an ongoing conversation. "What? I changed my mind."

The autonomous, independent obsession was exhausted and worn out. It was time to move on and create a new story that was more congruent with where I was in my life, where I desired and needed to go. What I deserved. It was time to get current. Conditions change, time passes, goals are reached, and what worked yesterday may be today's speed bump.

After considerable thought and deliberation, I, along with some very pointed coaching from a trusted friend, made a different choice. It is timely and more appropriate. Autonomy and independence have been put out to pasture. Occasionally, their curiosity interrupts their grazing to look up to see if I am making progress with my new story. I am currently riding the *intimacy* horse. Giddy yap! It has been a long, and at times, an uncomfortable mount. I frequently fall off and find myself staring at the underbelly of this new graceful gelding. What a different perspective. Unfamiliar hoof marks sporadically appear on my anatomy. This is brand-new territory to consider and explore. I long for my old story because it was such a valuable and familiar friend. It was my *"Hi Ho Silver."* I had it mastered, but it grew old and was headed for the glue factory.

Intimacy is now the compass setting. I have a new bride as my mentor, lots of embedded learning to draw upon and an awakened awareness as my guiding shepherd. "I'd love to have a tuna sandwich. Thank you very much. Would you like for me to make you one also?" (This is hard!)

Give it up if it is not working. In the past 15 years, I have heard hundreds of stories from leaders of small to midsize businesses describing who they were and what they were all about. They were insightful and periodically accurate. Maybe, at one time, you needed to be a hard-nosed, driving SOB to accelerate you to your current destination. That story may have run its course. Check it out. Delegating and empowerment might be better and wiser choices. You make the decision. After all, it is your company. It is your net worth!

I was recently speaking to a TEC Group in the Midwest. The TEC facilitator asked a prospective new member who was attending the meeting to choose one word that best described him on the job. Don, the candidate, did not hesitate for a second and proudly announced to a room of new acquaintances, "I'm an asshole." A long silence followed his unanticipated blurt. Incoming! Something foul had been lobbed into the group's punchbowl.

The existing members quickly exchanged wide-eyed glances with one another as the air attempted to re-enter the room. I thought, "This is going to be interesting." It was! Don's self-assessment proved to be on target as we experienced him throughout the rest of the session. He interrupted, argued, side talked and took a disproportionate amount of airtime. The group elected to decline on his membership. TEC is for healthy CEOs and companies. Be careful how you depict yourself. You just might become what you claim to be.

Evaluate, calibrate, and trust the evidence suggesting that what you are doing needs adjusting or not. Where are you on your personal and professional bell-shaped curve? What is effective and what is not?

Bless your old story because it was a treasured comrade, who proved tremendously valuable in transporting you to where you currently are. If no longer appropriate, put it to rest. An appropriate and respectful eulogy is in store. With arms and heart wide open, welcome the new version of you. You are simply accessing another part of yourself. It was there all along. No need to take a course. It is your ticket on your Greyhound bus bound to where you need and deserve to go.

For many years, I facilitated marketing events for TEC. The organization would mass mail to CEOs in a given market an invitation to attend a breakfast or lunch and learn about this valuable resource for business leaders. I would host these gatherings and in a 90-minute slot, the TEC story would be told and set the stage for enrollment into a specific TEC Group. What was astounding was that TEC would invite CEOs to attend the functions and people kept showing up. Go figure.

Shakespeare said, "God has given us one face, yet we put on another." Resist the temptation. The more consistent and predictably authentic you are, the more you will influence your organization. You advertise for controllers, salespeople, administrators, and human beings keep coming to your door seeking employment and relationships. They crave to be led by other human beings, and you cannot accomplish that by insisting on being someone else. Wear that one original face well.

Review: To be a successful and effective leader of a small to midsize business you must:

1. **Be who you are and not who you think should be.**
2. **Bring your best self forward and change what is not working.**
3. **Individualize and give permission for others to do the same.**
4. **Update your "story"; your old one may be obsolete.**

Robust actions to take:

1. Write five adjectives/nouns that best describe the ideal CEO/leader.

2. Write five adjectives/nouns that best describe you (negative and positive) as a CEO/leader.

3. What are the similarities and what are the differences?

4. If there are differences, what do you need to let go of and/or access to be in more alignment with the ideal CEO/ leader?

5. What are some of your behaviors that get in your way of leading your business?

6. What price are you paying for continuing those behaviors?

7. What are you willing to do about this?

8. What is your greatest fear of revealing who you really are to others?

9. What prices are you paying by withholding yourself?

10. What is one action you can take to bring more of yourself to your employees and organization?

11. What is your story?

12. Is it still serving you well or is it worn out?

13. If worn out, what is the story you would like others to tell about you?

14. What is one action you can immediately take to move toward that story?

Chapter Two

STRATEGY TWO: TAKE CARE OF YOURSELF FIRST, THEN OTHERS

Don't compromise yourself.
You are all you've got.

—Janice Joplin

Take the garbage out daily.

As the leader, it is 24/7. It is damn relentless. I suspect that you are not aware of the pressure and stress that you absorb on a daily basis leading your organization. I have objectively stood in the wings and observed all that you do. From my perspective, it is overwhelming. You hire and fire employees, negotiate loans, make sales calls, review financials, coach key reports, give reviews, run meetings, confront poor performance, cut deals, sign contracts, have difficult conversations with customers, vendors, bankers, lawyers and employees. That was all before lunch. These activities plus other factors that you bring from home can consciously or unconsciously contribute stress to your system. Your stress bucket is getting full and starting to overflow. Beware. You are entering the stress-overload danger zone.

Visualize a straightened paperclip being bent back and forth. If you do this enough times what happens? It eventually breaks into two pieces. The question is what bend caused it to break? The answer is all of them as the accumulation of stress on the paperclip weakened it to the point of coming apart. You might encounter a similar experience with your version of being bent daily time-and-time again.

One day you might come apart brought on by a weakened and completely saturated system. There you are out in front, bit in the mouth running on empty, faced with leading a dynamic and demanding business. Not a pretty picture or circumstance to be in. Do this. Journal your activities on any given business day and then review what you have logged. I will bet that you will be flabbergasted with the volume of activities that you have chosen to be involved with. Yes, I said chosen. We will talk about delegating later on.

If you accumulate stress on a daily basis then it seems reasonable to discover appropriate means to release it at the same frequency. I have asked thousands of business leaders what they do to release stress and tension from their lives and, in return, I receive an alarming high percentage of blank stares and concerned looks. A former TEC member in my group, when asked this question replied, "I go home every night and get shit-faced." Not exactly what I had in mind, but if that works who is to argue?

Stress reduction takes many forms. Whatever works for you is the right thing to do.

Strategies that I have heard are:

- "I run four miles everyday after work."
- "I listen to classical music before I go to bed."
- "I go home and dig in my garden."
- "I pray or meditate."
- "I sit down with my wife and talk about our day."
- "I take a 20-minute nap in mid-day."
- "I play the piano."
- "I just dumb down in front of the television."
- "I don't do squat."

That last one is frightening. Again, do whatever works, but please do something and do it often if not daily. Do not remain stationary, absorbing every punch straight on the chin and delude yourself that this strategy will suffice. It will not. You are a time bomb if you ignore this or play dumb. It is extremely difficult to run a business from an intensive care unit. Everyone deserves better—especially you.

The argument I often hear is that "I don't have the time to de-stress or shoehorn one more activity in my demanding calendar," or, "I can handle it." I am not buying that. It is not about time or the ability to deal with anything. It is about priorities and commitment. Be smart. You know you are. Some of you take better care of your import luxury automobile than you do yourself. When the red light comes on in that puppy, you pull over right now and get assistance! Let us preempt and head this off before the warning light suddenly appears on your computerized dash and you are between rest stops.

Robert is the CEO of a $20 million manufacturing company. He is a consummate micro-manager who insists on being in on everything that his company does. He is unreasonably driven and considers himself a real man who can effectively deal with anything that the world hands him. It is what he bi-laterally decided is the truth about himself with the assistance of his father. It is his story and he stuck to it far too long. Delegation, trust, and empowerment were foreign concepts to him. At least they were until he snapped and was shackled by inertness. The 14-hour work days, the lack of sleep, eating on the run, the stored anxiety, the interruptions in his day and the lack of any release mechanism finally caught up with him. He ignored the signals that he was rocketing toward a black hole, got a severe case of target fixation, and bored himself and his company in a crater.

Harvey Wiley, legendary New York boxing icon commenting on fighting Ali: "Things just went sour gradually all at once. He'll pick you and peck you, peck you and pick you, until you don't know where you are." That is what happened to Robert. There was a constant "rat-a-tat-tat" on his internal well being that he ignored. Denial was his mantra. Woody Woodpecker was embedded on his forehead pecking away at his financial, mental, emotional, and physical health. Justification was easy and familiar. The price he paid was difficult and unexpected.

Robert is now spending what used to be his equity-building time in therapy and rehabilitation clinics trying to comprehend how this all happened, learning how to delegate and ultimately reclaim his life. The company is on financial and emotional life support while he recovers. Remember what doctors are taught in medical school; do no harm, especially to yourself. Get the picture?

Be selfish and satisfy your, "what if."

I will wager that you have read somewhere or heard someone that you thought was smarter than you say that you should be a "servant leader," that the customer is "always right," that you should have an "open door" policy in your business, that the "buck stops here." Enough already! I understand the concepts, but I have observed so many of you taking all of this to such an extreme. You wind up with too much on your overcrowded plate, attempting to please an ever expanding and demanding internal and external community.

Some of you do this because you truly believe it is the right thing to do or it is all you know. You might have a high need to be liked or you concluded that you have no other choice. Maybe your dad or mom did it this way or you fear confrontation and saying "no" to employees, customers, vendors, and the other people that you deal with. In the years working with and listening to leaders of small to midsize organizations, I have heard it all. Here is the deal. If you do not take care of yourself, *depleted and cheated* is going to be your middle name. At the end of the day, you are going to feel physically and emotionally exhausted and, on some conscious or unconscious level, ripped off.

My best friend lives in Spokane, Washington. I met Frank (his nickname is "Ginge") in 1963 as a freshman at the University of Washington. We were talented football players on full scholarships, competing for the same position and living in rival fraternities. With that as our launching pad, over the past four decades we nurtured a friendship that has never wavered. I absolutely have come to love this wonderfully devoted friend.

About 10 years ago, I received a telephone call from Ginge. He was calling from a prone position in a New York City hospital recovering from a ruptured colon, emergency surgery and missing 18 inches of his lower intestine. He was groggy, considerably lighter and nearly died from the incident. It was a wakeup call prompting him to reflect on how he wanted to live his second half. One of the issues regarded our friendship. He wanted more face-to-face time with his best friend. Ginge asked for us to make a commitment to one another that each year we would go someplace and just hang out, play golf, eat great meals, reminisce about the past and peek into each other's future. No kids, no spouses, no other friends. No permission granted from anyone except us. I agreed, and we have been going on annual excursions for the past decade and we will continue to do so even when our luggage starts to include bedpans, walkers and various plug-in transparent tubes. It is just for us.

I suspect others might view these getaways as selfish and self-serving. I do not experience it that way. My annual adventures with Ginge are mentally, emotionally, physically, and spiritually healthy. The time with my best friend is richly rewarding, filling me to the top. I believe that I deserve a break at minimum once a year. Following the retreats, it requires a few days to deprogram the locker room language, but that is the only drawback.

Reward yourself. You are so accustomed to taking care of others that you often exclude yourself. Declare something just for you and act upon it with the same vigor and attention that you do when meeting other people's needs.

Buy that Harley and take motorcycle-driving lessons. Float the Colorado with some friends from college. Have a night out playing poker, going shopping. Take a nap in the middle of the day. Go to the gym at noon. Take piano lessons. Write your book. Whatever makes you happy and fulfilled should be your guide to the activity. Is it not possible that if you do something for yourself others also might benefit?

I fear that some of you may experience a "what if" conversation with yourself when it is too late to do anything about it. You know, "what if I had only." Nobody wants or deserves to have that exchange with themselves or with their loved ones.

Terry was a TEC member in his mid-forties. He was self-made, rose from the trades and eventually created a multi-million dollar business building custom homes for professionals in his community. He was not what you would call "a great businessman," but he was sound, honest, smart, a learner, and giving it all he had. I was proud to have him in my TEC Group and call him my friend.

One morning Terry slipped out of bed, meandered into the bathroom to shave, looked into the mirror above the sinks, and stopped breathing. Staring back at him was an unfamiliar and concerned face. His skin was dark yellow as if someone during the night had snuck into his bedroom and painted him the color of a caution light. He called out for his wife Barbara to come and look. She did and then rushed to the telephone to call their family doctor to find out what was happening to her husband.

Terry was able to go in that morning to see the doctor because of their friendship (try that today in a metropolitan area). It was not good news as an afternoon exploratory surgery revealed pancreatic cancer ravaging his body in an advanced and unstoppable stage. He had perhaps three to four months on the planet and that was it. It was a devastating blow for everyone involved in Terry's life.

Over the next three months, Terry made every effort to attend the monthly TEC meetings. He was exhausted, losing weight, in considerable pain and could only manage to be with his business colleagues for a few hours of the all-day meeting. The time he spent with us was invaluable in helping us reset what was important in our lives. Yes, we were business people and owners of successful businesses, but we also had families, friends, hobbies, and a life to be fully lived with robust passion and self-initiated fulfillment. Terry was firm and relentless with his message. It was a call to duty for everyone in the room. He had and deserved our attention.

On a Sunday morning approximately four months following the diagnosis, I received a call from Barbara requesting that I immediately come to their house. I knew what this meant and had been dreading this private invitation for weeks. Terry was not going to be with us much longer.

Upon arriving at their home, Barbara pointed to the upstairs bedroom where Terry, in a hospice situation, was resting. She appeared worn and distant. This stalwart woman had absorbed a heavy toll and was doing all that she could to work through the issues around Terry's eventual fate. She had remained strong and a focal point for friends, family, and business associates throughout the entire ordeal. There was no need to say anything. The communication was exquisite.

As I walked up the steps to the master bedroom, I began shaking and feeling more frightened than any other time in my life. I was certain I would fall apart, say the wrong thing, or just lose it in front of a person who deserved so much more of me in this moment. When I entered the room and encountered Terry for the first time in a couple of weeks, I gasped at how weak and small he had become. His "Popeye" forearms reduced to slender willows, his handsome face drawn and stretched taut across his cheekbone, his strong, powerful body now frail and a fraction of what he had been. He noticed my discomfort and whispered in a frail hoarse voice, "Come in, Ole. I promise I won't do anything drastic in the next couple of hours. Lay beside me so you can hear. I have a few things I want to talk about."

Terry thanked me for what I had contributed to his life, how I had helped him with the business and how I had been a good and faithful friend. I became less fearful and more engaged in this most important conversation as I listened and remained attentively still laying next to him. It was a sacred moment and deserved my fullest attention.

"I have one more thing to say," Terry continued looking more fatigued than when I first came in, his voice becoming weaker, and his pace considerably slower. "I know that you speak to my business colleagues, people like me all over the world, and I have a message that I would like for you to pass on to them."

"Of course I will. Anything. What is it?"

"Please tell them to never, never subordinate to their business anything that they believe is really important to them.

Business is only one part of who we are. Ole, this thing consumed me. I think I knew it at the time but I just ignored what was happening. I never seemed to get to the stuff that was vital to my life and happiness. I mean my family, health, hobbies, friendships, you know. Do you get what I am saying?"

I nodded hoping that he knew I understood and softly asked, "What stuff didn't you get to, Terry? What didn't you pay attention to?"

Tears welling in his eyes, his voice becoming more faint, Terry replied, "I never took the time to be Geppetto."

"What?"

"I didn't stand shoulder to shoulder with Pinocchio, you know, my son David, together crafting beautiful wood furniture with *our* hands. I had the tools and the skill. We could have spent wonderful time one-on-one. *The Field of Dreams* father and son, playing catch until dark. It could have been our version. I could have left him with that experience and skill. He could have remembered me for that. Now it is too late. I can't even hold a tool let alone stand shoulder to shoulder with anyone. He doesn't really know me and I don't really know him the way I should have and wanted to."

"Have you told David what you just shared with me?"

"Yes, yesterday. I told him that I deeply loved him and that I did the best that I could. He said he understood. It was hard and I'm not sure he got it."

Terry had just told me his "what if." He was current with David. My guess is that David did get it and will always remember his dad the way Terry wanted him to.

My friend and client passed away shortly after that conversation, embraced and comforted by his family and best friend in the TEC Group. Most of his fellow TEC members attended the memorial and were there to say farewell to our fallen comrade. We had lost a member of the tribe. Some could not handle it and stayed away. Terry would understand.

For the next 12 months, the TEC Group kept a conference table place setting along with his name tent for Terry at the monthly meeting to honor him and to remind all of us to live a more balanced and more fulfilling life. To make sure that our priorities were in proper order. People come and go in our lives, and when they go they leave the best of themselves behind with us.

Pay attention. One day one of you may go to the mirror to shave or put on makeup and a stranger may be staring back at you suggesting that there is very little time left to do the things in your life that are really important. Like the old saying goes, in the last moments nobody ever writes on their tombstone that they wished they had spent more time at the office.

Thank you, Terry, for this reminder. God bless you and safe journey, my friend.

Master the balancing act.

I firmly believe that you can stay in the fast lane for a significant amount of time if you create a high degree of balance in your life. You are more than a leader of a successful business. The problem is that most of you identify with only one facet of yourself, the businessperson. "I am a business person," you publicly declare unconsciously limiting many other possibilities in your life. You are much more. Previously stated, you are a spouse, parent, an athlete and have many other dimensions of yourself to explore and expand. Keep in mind that you are a holistic spiritual being who on occasion runs a prospering business. What if you approached all of the non-business areas of your life with the same enthusiasm and attention that you do when working in or on the business? What would that be like?

Be honest with yourself. What are you doing about your relationships, your finances, your health, your spiritual life, your personal interests, your family and all those other facets of your existence that comprise your total life? Is it not true that at times we need to reset these areas? Habits, staleness, and familiarity can set in and dull our experience. I know that you spend most of your energy and time focusing on the business, but at what cost? I do not blame you. I am not here to pass judgment. I would probably do the same thing if it were not for all the observations and knowledge I have accumulated in the past 17 years working with you in the trenches. You have been extraordinary teachers.

Here is the deal. If you had more balance in your life I believe you could perform at a much higher level in your business. And if your business improves, you have more time and resources to broaden your experience of your life and around and around it goes. It does not have to be a paradox. Ease into it by starting to dilute your business activities and see yourself in a more holistic way. You do not have to dive into the deep end. Wade out from the shallow end one step at a time.

I have never encountered a population of people that is better at creating tangible results (money or what money can buy) than you. You have figured this one out. Nice going. You live in a world of abundance, and it is perfectly acceptable to cast the net and haul in the catch. You deserve as much of it as you can constructively acquire. An issue with you is: when is enough, enough and when does this get out of balance with the intangible (values, purpose, behaviors, spiritual) side of your life?

Your competitive nature gets in the way. You build up a net worth of $X and you find out that a competitor, country club member or colleague has $Y and off you go, bit in mouth again, lathered up, streaking to the lead. This can be healthy if what you are doing to create the tangible success also brings you fulfillment and allows you to participate in other aspects of your life. Without that fulfillment or variety, you can run out of gas, having plenty of toys, but nobody to play with. Deep down, where you live, that is not what you want. Remember . . . he who dies with the most toys still dies and somebody else gets the toys or winds up squabbling over them.

My wife, Sue Ann, and I live in a vast golf complex, with multiple courses, clubhouses, workout facilities, in Southern California. During our first month in our new home in this golfing community, we were excited about playing all of the courses and meeting the existing members. One day we scheduled a tee time at one of the links that we had not previously played. It was early in the morning and a picture-perfect day for golf. As we drove up to the first tee box in our golf cart, the starter came over, welcomed the two of us, and asked if we would be willing to play in a threesome with one of the members of the club who was looking for a game.

"Terrific," I thought, "a chance to meet someone new who was also familiar with the golf course that we were playing. A win-win for all of us."

The starter introduced Sue Ann and I to the member. He shook our hands and handed me his business card. I thought that was unusual but, wanting to be courteous, I took the card, read it and was surprised to see that on the business card was a color picture of this member standing beside a Lear Jet. I concluded, "aha," he must be in the aviation business. Turning the card over I discovered he owned a company that manufactured bearings for heavy equipment. It was impossible not to notice that his golf cart was different from the "vanilla" cart we owned. His was a candy-apple red custom miniature Jaguar with a CD deck, an overhead cooling system, a hands-free telephone system and dark leather seats. Harnessed on the back of his golf cart was the most expensive golf bag and set of state-of-the-art clubs I have ever seen. To top it off, our new playing partner was dressed exquisitely head to toe in the latest golf attire.

As we approached the tee box on number one he asked, "Would you like to make this interesting?"

"Eh, sure," I replied. "What do you have in mind?"

"How about a buck a hole, and a five dollar bonus for lowest net."

"You're on," my competitive monster reared up and replied. "Woman, into the cart. The game is on." After doing the handicap bookkeeping and adjusting, off we went.

We were playing even until I got on a hot streak and started to win some holes on the back nine. He was becoming more irritated as I teed off first on three consecutive holes. We were standing at the number-15 tee box, a par five with a blind first shot over a hill. I asked, "Any trouble over the hill?"

"Nope, no trouble," he offered, "Blast away!"

I did and when I drove my cart over the hill for my second shot, I discovered the lake. No ball in sight and not even a ripple was present where the golf ball had entered the water. No trouble for him as he hit a five iron off the tee to the crest of the hill and was bone dry for his second shot.

I challenged him on his advice and he brusquely replied, "We are playing for money. This is a competition and you should have done your homework. It's your responsibility to know what you're getting into." I was astonished, settled on the spot and drove to the clubhouse. "Have a nice day."

Maybe he was a bit too focused on the tangible side of his life. Maybe he was slightly out of balance. Maybe he did not know any better. Maybe he was just a jerk. In any event, you can still find that member at the number-one tee box on all the courses with one bag on the back of his golf cart looking for a game.

Stretch and go beyond comfort.

Michelangelo said, "The greatest danger for most of us is not that our aim it is too high and we miss it, but that it is too low and we reach it." It has been my experience that most of you have only a limited view of what you can actually accomplish. I suspect that you are using only a small percentage of your potential. Do not get me wrong. You have achieved at a level that few can only imagine or, perhaps, more accurately, cannot imagine. The question is: what is getting in your way to access more of your potential in both your personal and professional life?

We can all conjure up our own reasons and excuses. Here are a few I have heard:

- "This is all I want out of life."
- "I got tired."
- "I didn't know that those other parts of me existed."
- "I've done better than most people."
- "I settled into a comfort zone."
- "I ran out of money, time and energy."
- "I don't deserve more."
- "I'm an imposter."
- "I just lucked out."
- "I don't know how to take my life to the next level."

All are valid explanations and your reality is truly your reality. You own it. I respect that. Maybe the more valid answer lies in the fact that what you did to be successful in business never transferred to your personal life. You never became aware of the process so you could deliberately replicate it and teach others. Again, what I am attempting to do is to widen your life's band and have you experience yourself at an expanded and balanced level. You deserve it.

Here are the steps I would wager that you are taking to be a successful businessperson, and I guarantee you they will work equally well in your personal life.

Step One: You have great clarity about what you want to do in your life.
Low performance people use confusion as a strategy for staying stuck.

Step Two: You have the ability to sense the future and move toward your fresh pictures, thoughts, and emotions.
Low performance people focus on the past, allowing outdated pictures, thoughts, and emotions to determine their future.

Step Three: Your inner dialogue is positive about yourself and about life in general.
Low performance people have a negative inner dialogue about themselves and life.

Step Four: Your emotions are positive regarding your future and yourself.
Low performance people's emotions are negative.

Step Five: You embrace a high degree of accountability and self-efficacy.
Low performance people embrace a high degree of subordination and helplessness.

Step Six: You are real about your life.
Low performance people are in denial and fantasy.

Step Seven: You work diligently and with intelligence. You pay the price through sacrifice, delaying gratification, and doing whatever it morally takes to get the job done.

Low performance people believe the world owes them comfort and success.

Martin is in his early sixties. He is a TEC member in a California group. I spoke to Martin and his fellow CEOs about seven years ago, and much of the material that I covered dealt with balance and implementing the seven steps in all aspects of one's life.

Seven years ago, Martin had figured out how to be relatively successful in business. He had provided financial security for him and his family but had reached a plateau. Martin was starting to slide down the other side of his professional bell-shaped curve. The rest of his life was mediocre at best. He was not in the best of health. He had limited energy. His relationship with his wife was becoming stale. He did not have many friends, and life was becoming dull and predictable. Conversations were becoming redundant with little new ground being explored. His enthusiasm for life was waning. He had not tried anything new in his life for a decade or so and was beginning to think that "this is all there is."

I recently returned to talk to this group at a retreat with their spouses and reacquainted myself with Martin. The material was essentially the same as before except for new stories and a slightly different emphasis. I was surprised to find that he was still a member of that TEC group and evidently had either broken through the doldrums of seven years ago or was just hanging on. Just before one of the breaks in the seminar, Martin raised his hand and asked if he could share something important with the rest of the group. I, curious as to what he had in mind, said fine.

"I'm not here to promote Ole Carlson, but I have to tell you this guy that we have in front of us literally saved my life."

"Ah come on Martin, I protested, but please do continue for as long as you'd like."

"When Ole first spoke to this group some time ago I was in the tank. You guys remember that? Well, I am here to tell you that this stuff works. It's not magical, mystical or rabble babble psycho bullshit. It is simply the way life can work for you and me if we put it to use. By implementing this material, everything in my life changed for the better and I have never felt better about myself or about what I have accomplished. That's the damn truth! I am a living, breathing, testimonial turnaround and it was all because I did what Ole is suggesting."

Please notice again. We seldom are aware of when we are facilitating someone's personal and professional transformation. Evidently, Martin concluded that there was a lot more to life and he had only scratched the surface of what could be for him. Martin spoke with conviction, renewed energy, and enthusiasm. His wife beamed while he talked about their relationship. He spoke passionately about the growth and profitability in his business, about taking it to another level by bringing in new talent and changing his micro-manager ways. He had reacquainted himself with dusty and seemingly worn-out friends and had brought new people into his life. He was working out at the gym and physically feeling better than at any other time that he could recall. His spiritual life was rejuvenated and more in congruence with his current station in life. He had done all of this by himself armed with only the seven basics of creating a rewarding and fulfilling reality. That was all he really needed. I firmly believe that deep down inside we know what to do. Get the ball rolling and get out of the way.

Here comes the preacher. Do not settle. You are much more than what you are experiencing. Take it to the limit. Horizons are waiting to be sailed over. You are special because you are in the chair of the leader of a successful business. As a percentage of the population, not many people can do what you have done. Digest, accept, and give yourself credit. If it feels right, if you believe it is right for you, take it up a notch in all areas of your life. Your business will benefit as you expand and widen your experience of this unique person called you.

Review: To be a successful and effective leader of a small to midsize business you must:

1. Take the garbage out daily.
2. Be selfish and avoid the "what if."
3. Master the balancing act.
4. Stretch and go beyond comfort.

Robust actions to take:

1. For one workweek journal all of the activities that you are involved in on a daily basis. Do not censor, and please include everything whether it seems stressful or not. Rate each activity on a scale of 1 to 5 with 1 being the least stressful and 5 being the most stressful. Pay special attention to the 5's. Identify what you are doing on a daily basis to relieve the stress, and if there is not any activity, choose one that allows you to drain the accumulated tension from your system.

2. Write down what you have done for yourself in the past six months that was just for you. If the list is short or nonexistent, decide right now to declare something. Approach this activity as if it really mattered and with the same robust passion and interest that you do when taking care of others. This is a non-negotiable contract with you. Make a commitment to honor it no matter what.

3. Declare one goal in each of the following categories that you will achieve in the next 12 months.

Financial:

My goal is to _____

My obstacle is _____

My robust first step is to _____

Spiritual:

My goal is to _____

My obstacle is _____

My robust first step is to _____

Personal:

My goal is to _____

My obstacle is _____

My robust first step is to _____

Health:

My goal is to _____

My obstacle is _____

My robust first step is to _____

Relationships:

My goal is to _____

My obstacle is _____

My robust first step is to _____

4. Identify and commit to unreasonably reset yourself in all areas of your life. Examine where you have fallen asleep and give yourself a wake-up call. 911. You deserve it, the people in your life deserve it, and I guarantee that once you become fully awake again your life will dramatically change for the better.

Chapter Three

Strategy Three: Lead the Organization, Let Others Manage It

*A leader should not get too far in front of his troops or
he will be shot in the ass.*

—Joseph Clark

Own being the leader.

Whether you signed up for it or not, you are it. It does not matter what package you come in, male or female, tall or short, young or old, obese or rail thin, articulate or tongue-tied, experienced or an unsure rookie, your "job" as the leader in your organization is to:

- Inspire, influence, and transform your people.

- Set the corporate compass with your vision.
- Be decisive.
- Drive the business with *your* principles.
- Delegate, then get busy doing what you are paid to do.

I have the honor of working worldwide with thousands of successful leaders of small to midsize businesses. This is what I am learning about them. They have the ability to attract and lead talented followers. When they turn around, they see a column forming behind them of mostly familiar faces and occasionally some strangers attempting to crowd in the queue.

They are able to explicitly communicate to the organization where they want to go and to motivate their direct report managers to get them to that destination and far beyond. I believe this is what effective leadership is all about. The above short list represents a proven road map to high achievement and can be your formula for continued success in your business.

Let us keep it simple so you do not become overwhelmed and bogged down trying to sort through what it is you are expected to do. There is an abundance of written and recorded material telling you how to become a better leader. Most of it is sound, expert advice. It is not like we are in a vacuum of information regarding the subject. Investigate what is out there. Select what works for you, and above all else, follow the proven advice and methods of your peers who appreciate and understand what it is like to be in your shoes. You can trust this tribe like no other. It is a credible bunch.

Inspire, influence, and transform your people.

You are the only person in your organization able to infiltrate the organizational chart at all levels and cross all functional boundaries with no limitations and no border guards. Understand that you cannot do that sitting in your soft leather chair behind a closed door pouring over a spreadsheet or reading the *Wall Street Journal*. Consistently walk the extremities of the building and get to know your people.

When I was a freshman pledge in the Phi Delta Theta fraternity at the University of Washington, the upperclassmen insisted that I get to know the brothers. There were fines and spats if you did not know their names. Same thing applies here. Make yourself visible and leverage the fact that you have an almost godlike impact on the people who work for you. O.K., maybe deity status is overstating the truth. However, at the very least, you have parental rank and that is good enough to make a significant difference in someone's life. One good word from you goes a long way, and like I said a couple of times (do you might think that I believe this is important?), we never know when we are facilitating another person's transformation.

David Whyte, the English author and poet, was the featured keynote speaker at TEC International's 1999 Annual Conference. He held the audience spellbound as he wove sound business principles with his original poetry and stories. He left TEC International leaders a new language and a fresh, new way to view their role with their members.

The leadership at TEC International believed that David and I would make a good team and complement one another. We agreed and I designed a three-day personal transformation workshop that highlighted David for one of the three days. Our venue was the perennial five-star Broadmoor Resort and Spa in Colorado Springs, Colorado. Not bad. Our audience was comprised of executives from TEC International and TEC facilitators. It was a magical three days in a wondrous Rocky Mountain setting. Does it get any better than that? David shared with the group a poem he had written that captures what people, who happen to be employees, want, and desire, in this fast-moving, post-modern business environment.

Loaves and Fishes
By David Whyte

This is not
the age of information.
This is not
the age of information.
Forget the news,
and the radio,
and the blurred screen.
This is the time
of loaves and fishes.
People are hungry,
and one good word is bread
for a thousand.
—*from* The House of Belonging

I noticed that one of my clients never complimented or verbally rewarded his employees. When I challenged him on his behavior he replied, "I'll be damned if I'll ever say something good to any of them about them because my dad never said anything good to me about me." How is that for logic? Eventually I found him to be trainable and have encouraged him to enroll in a 12-step recovery program designed to "get over it" and if for nothing else pass on a few "atta persons" for business reasons. This is low hanging fruit that does not cost a penny and has an infinite return. Invest!

Albert Einstein said, "Only a life lived for others is worth living." Admittedly, Albert was one of the sharpest knives in the 20th Century drawer and I respect his opinion. However, I would like to rein that in just a hair. I believe Albert's stance in life can be taken to an unproductive extreme (see Chapter

Two). I struggle with stretching the "servant leader" model to the outermost exhausting boundaries. Identify and focus on the top 20% of your people and devote 80% of your time and resources furthering them along. The bottom feeders might get the joke and some of them could possibly rise above where they are currently resting and hiding (and they are resting and hiding, do not kid yourself). Do not spend your valuable time trying to elevate those floundering around and stuck ankle deep in foul-smelling corporate sediment. Stay with your winners and demonstrate to them how to get to where you currently are and to where you are headed. That is being a leader.

When I was working directly with CEOs while with The Executive Committee, I would meet for two hours once a month with each member of my TEC Group. That was 16 appointments every month come rain or shine, sickness or conflicting tee times. It was an essential and differentiating element of the TEC model. We referred to the meetings as "one-to-ones." The sessions were scheduled, closed-door, confidential and at times very intense get-togethers where the member and I explored what he or she was working on, whether they were stuck or not, where they were going and all other topics that really mattered in their personal and professional lives and wanted to avoid talking about. We sparred back and forth from a prepared agenda, and at the conclusion of the meeting, the member committed to certain actions that would accelerate him or her forward. High level listening, relentless clarifying and resisting offering sage advice were the main skills that were demanded of me. I learned how to listen objectively without judgment or blame. Try that. It is not as easy a task as it may seem. Some of the conversations frightened the highly paid consultant out of me and I wanted to scream out with veins popping on my forehead, "Are you out of your ever-loving freaking mind?" Nevertheless, I remained poker-faced, heart pounding and kept exploring. Try that! When appropriate I held their feet to the fire.

Most successful TEC members replicated the "one-to-one" exercise with their corporate keepers. It was a process allowing them to develop their top 20%, and to spend quality, uninterrupted time with the people who were responsible for increasing the majority shareholder's net worth. I wholeheartedly recommend that you do the same. You need more face-to-face time with your winners.

Rising stars want to learn and grow. It is their hunger and they are voracious consumers. Do not tell me you do not have the time or they would not be interested. You do and they are! Keep in mind that the more they increase their personal inventory of skills, knowledge and experience the more valuable they become in a free agent business environment to you and to others (more on that later). It is the "others" that you should be most concerned with. Top people understand and are eager to implement this personal advancement strategy. I do not blame them. Stay engaged. Lassoing talented people is an ongoing challenge. Other interested people with resources equal to or exceeding yours are talking with them over expense account dinners and extra dry, two olive martinis, offering them opportunities that they may find difficult to refuse.

Aggressive recruiters are actively pursuing industry stars. I was speaking at a banking conference about the free agent situation and someone in the audience raised his hand in utter frustration and shouted, "I'm damn sick and tired of these blasted flesh peddlers calling into my organization hustling my top people." Before I could respond someone else in the audience shouted out, "You should be more concerned when they stop calling!" Good point.

It seems to be a classic "Catch 22." You are investing your money, time, experience, and wisdom in developing your key people, and one day, off they go to start their own company, perhaps even competing directly against you. Consider this; they could be your successor and an integral and only participant in your exit strategy. They might become a valuable customer or have some other future strategic relationship or alliance with you and your company. While you have them, they may accelerate your company to heights you never considered or had the ability to accomplish. Enjoy them while you can.

Growing them is a sound business investment. When it is all said and done, you will know that you were instrumental in assisting another person in reaching out to live the quality of life that you created for yourself. Down deep, that is what you want. It is a form of "paying it forward." You will sleep well at night having accomplished that.

Use the "one-to-one" to *inspire* your top performers to go far beyond where they currently are. Assist them in creating a vivid picture of their future self. Share with them your journey. You are already there or nearly there. Show them the steps that you took, the speed bumps that you glided or bumped over, what to leverage, and what to discard. Do not assume that they know. They do not because if they did they would be in a seat similar to yours having this talk with their direct reports. Engage in a continuous conversation relative to their career path. Explore areas that they need to develop, skills they need to acquire, behaviors that would benefit them as they move forward in their careers. Provide them opportunities to stretch beyond immediate comfort, make resources available that they may need, and above all, remain active in the conversation.

We *influence* people through coaching, mentoring, and role modeling. The most important person to anyone in the workplace is his or her immediate boss. Leverage this position. According to our relativity friend Albert Einstein, "setting an example is not the main means of influencing another, it is the only means." You do not always have to be perfect but you had better understand that you are being watched and interpreted by your people day by day, hour by hour, minute by minute, second by second. You are in the fishbowl being magnified completely out of proportion. Be aware and beware. Show them what success looks, tastes, sounds, and feels like. Nudge them along and allow them to make their own mistakes and learn from their own experiences. Help them raise the bar on their performance by spending shoulder-to-shoulder time (Geppetto-like) with them passing on what you have learned.

Influence does not mean control. Once you intentionally control another person, you no longer influence at any significant level. Agree upon the objectives, set clear expectations, then get the hell out of the way. Learn to step in only when appropriate. Let go of your need to rescue.

Conrad Hilton suggests that, "Success seems to be connected with action. Successful people keep moving. They make mistakes, but they don't quit." Your duty is to keep the keepers moving along on their journey and refusing to let them quit. As Confucius said, "I hear and forget. I see and remember. I do and I understand."

We have in the "one-to-one" a perfect venue for facilitating *transformation*. We can make dreams visible for our employees who are temporarily asleep or blinded by repetitious, too familiar, and comfortable tasks. Mahatma Ghandi reminds us that, "A friend is someone who knows the song in your heart and can sing it back to you when you have forgotten the words." Look at every interchange with your key people as an opportunity to move them beyond where they currently stand or are stuck.

Conversations should be more than just an exchange of meaningless clichés or a habitual and mindless slapping of high fives. Sing the songs back to your stars. Challenge them to get involved with their own personal and professional evolution. Ultimately they should leave that encounter with you having learned something new, given a challenging assignment, received feedback that will propel them forward or correct ineffective behavior. And above all, wanting to come back for more. Be intentional with your conversations. It is an opportunity and responsibility that you must not take lightly. You have an obligation to grow the human currency along with the actual dollars in your business. You are perfectly positioned for this task. You are the leader. Hey, you might even learn something useful for yourself.

Be decisive. "Ever notice that "*what the hell*" is always the right decision?"

—Anonymous

I would think that most of you would agree that the velocity of change in the business environment is accelerating at an unprecedented rate. The economy may slow and speed up but the rate of change has the pedal to the metal. Penetrating change and the deluge of information has overwhelmed the current global business environment. I have observed many business leaders become frozen at the wheel trying to digest the avalanche of data cascading down upon their business, industry, and markets. Some have become obsessed in knowing all that they can possible know in order to make the perfect decision. Forget that notion. You cannot possibly adsorb it all. General George S. Patton Jr. said, "A good solution applied with vigor now is better than a perfect solution applied 10 minutes later." It is only going to get worse as no hand is reaching for the faucet. Give it up. Do not become an information junkie. Gather what you need and take action.

You no longer have the luxury of elaborately beta testing the South Sector for six months before you bring an idea to your market or company. Times have changed and are constantly changing. If you wait for all the compelling evidence to come in before you dramatically make a move, you will be witnessing your idea being brought into your market by a competitor who had a more expedient decision making process. Now more so than ever before decisiveness is king. From The Book of the Samurai by Hagakure comes this insight:

> *"In the words of the ancients one should make his decisions within the space of seven breaths. Lord Takanoba said, "If discrimination is long, it will spoil." Lord Naoshige said, "When matters are done leisurely, seven out of 10 will turn out badly. A warrior is a person who does things quickly." When your mind is going hither and thither, discrimination will never be brought to a conclusion. With an intense, fresh, and un-delaying spirit, one will make his judgment within the space of seven breaths. It is a matter of being determined and having the spirit to break through to the other side."*

I am experiencing many owners, CEOs, presidents and leaders actually holding their breath (forget about taking seven), hearts in their throats, lungs hyperventilating pushing the implement button and off they zoom. I find many highly successful entrepreneurs and rapidly rising companies in this group. Most thriving TEC members are bunched here. You need to be somewhat of a warrior, a modern-day Samurai. Everyday is "High Noon." You are Gary Cooper, in your corner office armed with modern technology, your intelligence, and your ability to make expedient decisions in an unstable business environment. If not, you should be.

When you find yourself off track you need to intervene early at the "easy stage." You can usually get back on track from that spot. If you allow matters to slide past the "easy stage" and hit the "crisis stage," you will be facing a long and nasty journey back to your original expectations. Your odds of getting there are slim, slight and not at all. The slide is caused by indecisiveness, a lack of enthusiasm, and a limited inventory of appropriate tools in confronting the issue.

When I was playing organized baseball my hitting coach made it simple. He told me simply to "see the ball and hit it." There was not time or space to intellectualize the situation or look at all the possible options. "Stay ahead in the count," he emphasized. The same fundamentals apply in this incident. See the problem, issue, situation, whatever, and deal with it in real time, otherwise you will fall behind in the count, and the advantage goes to the opponent. Ouch, strike three and you are out!

Whatever decision you make, major or minor, be certain that the implementers clearly understand what your expectations are. What specific outcomes do you want? It has been my experience that when projects, goals, tasks, strategies, assignments go off coarse, slide to the "crisis stage" or fail to reach completion, it is usually because the leader did not establish crystal-clear expectations with the people responsible for implementation.

Do not rely upon your direct reports to ask for explicit clarification. Many of them will not take that step for fear of looking foolish, ignorant or lacking the skills to complete the task. It is your responsibility to make certain that the people responsible for the completion of your edicts fully understand what it is you want them to do. Invest the time up front and do not assume that they know or should know. Asking them "are there any questions?" does not suffice. Have them play back to you what they heard. Go slow in your explanation of what it is you want. Ask them if they have ever done this type of work before, taken on these types of tasks in the past. Find out what resources they might need to be successful and provide them with what they requested. Do as thorough of a job as possible on the front end and you will find that the decisions and the assignments that you make will have a high success rate.

Talented, highly motivated people want to work for a leader who is decisive, who takes action, and who has forward accelerating momentum. Bottom feeders want to work for a "leader" who procrastinates, who mulls over decisions forever and is stuck. It is lonely at the bottom and they want company.

You make the choice; it is your net worth at risk.

Set the corporate compass with your vision.

We should agree upon what a "vision" actually is. I have been in numerous meetings with management teams where they cannot decide upon a commonly accepted definition. Much time is wasted with these unnecessary discussions. Some believe it is an elaborate tapestry that portrays all aspects of the company's future, others believe that it must be all encompassing, embellished with color, motion, sound, and texture. Many believe that it defines what an organization does relative to their employees, customers, vendors, board members, investors, local community, and anyone else that is remotely connected to the business. A few think it is something leaders and employees hallucinate over after far too many after-work cocktails, or perhaps they have had a personal encounter with one of the many deities roaming the Universe.

I like to keep things simple. A vision is a significant goal that you want the organization to reach at some point in the future. I prefer that it be specific and singular in nature. It is a BHAG. Put more explicitly; it is a big, hairy, audacious goal. Jack, while at GE, supposedly spawned that acronym, but I have used it so often I now falsely believe that I originated it. An example of a vision would be what John F. Kennedy declared in the early sixties relative to a staggering and faltering United States space program. His vision for the space program was to place a man on the moon and return him safely to earth by the end of the decade. It was specific, significant, and singular in nature—and it worked.

It is the leader's prerogative to unilaterally establish the vision and be able to change it without going through committees attempting to make certain that everyone in the organization agrees and feels good about it. If you do change the vision, be certain to inform your people so they are working on the correct initiatives. Do not outrun your headlights. You do not have the luxury of unproductive time pursuing every employee to build consensus. Besides, it is your company and your net worth.

I am constantly surprised that many leaders of organizations are content with just bumping their businesses along hoping to bang into something and subsequently identify it as their vision. "This is exactly where I wanted it to go and precisely what I had in mind," they exclaim to the gathering bewildered employee base. Nonsense! Productive people want to be led by decisive leaders who know where they want to go and are not afraid to declare their desires. Put your stake in the sand. Your most successful colleagues do.

Ralph Lauren believes that, "A leader has the vision and conviction that a dream can be achieved. He inspires the power and energy to get it done." That is called empowering and delegating. It is your dream and you need to enlist and motivate the troops in order to reach it. It is about the doing not just the declaring. Joel A. Barker states, "Vision without action is merely a dream. Action without vision just passes the time. Vision with action can change the world." From a small to midsize business lookout point, the world is a large place to impact, but I know you can influence what happens within the walls of your organization. I know you can significantly influence your segment of the market. I know with the proper vision and conviction you can make a difference regarding your net worth and financial security.

Learn to be consistently articulate. If people in your organization are chronically confused about where the business is going then there is only one nose to be pointed to. Yours! People interpret you and your actions through their own filters and perspective not yours. You had better make sure that they are hearing and seeing what you want them to hear and see. You might check in once in awhile instead of assuming they get it or waiting for a signal that they are headed for a deep and treacherous ditch.

Make certain that your lyrics (words), dance (body language), and melody (tone) are in exact alignment with the message that you are attempting to convey to your implementers. Be accountable for your words, actions, and demeanor. They are yours. Keep your message simple. Keep the conversation focused. Be the broadcaster. Yogi Berra was right when he said, "It was impossible to get a conversation going; everybody was talking too much." Keep the chatter at a minimum.

Most successful leaders are absolutely consistent and relentless in keeping their vision visible. Every encounter with their employees is an opportunity to embed their vision into the thinking and activities of the implementers. No gathering of employees is too small for their vision stump speech. No space is too sacred to escape the message about where they are going. You know you are about to reach saturation point when an employee sees you coming down the hall toward them and suddenly ducks into the nearest restroom. Gender is irrelevant. Follow them in, check for their feet under the stall door, knock and lay it on them one more time.

"Successful communication transforms your thoughts, will, and desire into action. It moves people. It transforms the thoughts, will, and desires of others. What better word for this process than magic?" says Jack Griffin, author of *How to Say It at Work*. Spin a little magic and see how pristine, persistent, and consistent you can make the communication of your vision.

Drive the business with *your* principles.

Elvis said, "Values are like fingerprints. Nobody's are the same, but you leave 'em all over everything you do." I have never considered *The King* to be much of a philosopher (You ain't nothing but a hound dog? What?), but I believe he captured what it is I want to say in this section. He is right. Many organizations choose to consciously and deliberately execute their principles when it is comfortable or convenient, but their fingerprints are left behind in all instances. In the end, organizations are known for what they stand for rather than for what they sell. Recently Enron, Tyco, WorldCom, and others appeared on the networks' six o'clock news. These behemoths of global commerce and their leaders will be remembered for what they slumped to, not for the products, goods or services they provided or the heights that they soared to. These embedded impressions have a long shelf life. Nobody is able to go back and entirely wipe clean the crime scene.

I want to share with you what successful leaders of small to midsize businesses are doing relative to this issue of principles and values. I witnessed this firsthand. There is not much wiggle room in this discussion and if I ever came close to declaring absolutes, this is it.

Almost absolute number one: This is your domain. The principles that you lead your organization with must be authored and originate from you. I do not believe this is a democratic process or should be sent to committees for a decision. It is your right to establish what you believe is appropriate for your business and not be held hostage to a group's declaration or desires. The principles that you hold dear propelled you to where you are today so they must work just fine. Make what you believe in highly visible. Be extremely explicit. Communicate, communicate, and above all else communicate.

Almost absolute number two: Remember you are in the fishbowl being constantly observed and critically judged. Below is a line from a song made popular by Sting.

> "Every move you make,
> every vow you break,
> every smile you fake,
> every claim you stake,
> I'll be watching you."

How true. So now, you are warned. It may not be fair but it is reality. Stay awake. Stay conscious. You must be impeccable in setting the example of how you want these principles and values lived and carried out. Screw up out of sight. If you are busted, fess up, do not cover up!

Almost absolute number three: Keep the principles few in number and high in impact. You are not in the behavior modification business. "Fuggetaboutit." You cannot successfully legislate the perfect employee. Keep it simple and decide what is really important and meaningful.

I was recruiting a prospective member to invite into my TEC Group. This CEO was successful, high profile and a fast tracker in the pharmaceutical industry. As I was waiting in the reception area of his business to meet with him, I could not help but notice the 10-foot by 10-foot value statement placard that was secured on his lobby wall. It was that enormous because he had posted 23 values that he expected his employees to adhere to. I thought to myself "slight overkill." When I met with the prospect, I mentioned to him that there were only Ten Commandments and we as a world community over the past 2000-plus years were having considerable difficulty implementing all of them to any acceptable degree and perhaps he could scale his back just a touch. He eventually did, and accepted the invitation to join the TEC Group.

Almost absolute number four: Live them always but especially in the following three instances.

- When you hire a new employee.
- When you witness them being lived.
- When you witness them being violated.

People walk into your organization with their own embedded software. Some prospective employees are team players—others may be lone wolves. Some are honest, some are crooks, and the list and possibilities goes on. If a cornerstone value in your organization is teamwork, you would be foolish to hire a lone wolf who blazes his or her own trail. You had better interview for the trait that you desire inside your walls. The odds suggest that the past is the best predictor of the future. Investigate if this prospective employee has this attribute and experience inside of him or her. If you hire someone with the wrong internal software and attempt to convert him or her, you will be subjected to something similar to a real software conversion. You know the drill. It will take longer than expected. It will cost more and it will not work as advertised. Be smart. Hire people who have the same values that you have.

When you witness the company values being lived by an employee or a group, make it visible. Call attention to it. Celebrate. Reinforce it. Broadcast the event to the rest of the organization. Do whatever is necessary in order to drive the message deep into the hearts, souls, and behaviors of the people in the business. You must be relentless in your effort. Posting the principles on some poster or screen saver and thinking that will steer the message home is naïve and unproductive.

Equally important is making visible in real time any violation of the principles. Turning your back on any erosion of what you hold as important diminishes what you believe in and says to the organization that these values and the implementation of them are arbitrary and optional. Believe in what you stand for and stand for what you believe in. You are not running a popularity contest, and if you have a high need to be liked and allow your employees to run roughshod over your values, you need to spend more time with your therapist.

Almost absolute number five: Use your principles as a filter for decision-making. This is your first cut regarding any choices or decisions that are made in your business by anyone in the business. It precedes strategic, economic, synergistic, logistic, and all other considerations. Roy Disney suggests, "It's not hard to make decisions when you know what your values are." These values create the crucible where the work takes place. The crucible must be solid, able to hold up under stress, enduring and above all else provide safe and predictable boundaries for people to do the work that you hired them to do.

Delegate . . . then get busy doing what you are being paid to do.

In year three of facilitating my TEC Group, the light bulb suddenly went on. The issues we were discussing in our all-day monthly meeting were management concerns not leadership topics. Duh! I had allowed the group to dumb down. I put this matter on the following month's agenda knowing that I was going to have to fall on the group leader's sword.

The next meeting came and the group and I had a frank discussion about how we were spending our time together and what we were bringing to the table to discuss and advise one another on. It was all about return on time and money. We concluded that the subjects that we were investing one another's time, money and intellect in were mostly items that should have been delegated to the member's management teams to solve and not be cluttering up the agenda of 15 leaders of fast-growing companies. I had a room full of carnivores and we were spending our valuable time chomping away on veggies and cream cheese. We were traveling along at ground level when we should have been soaring at 30,000 feet looking over the horizon.

Following our discussion a 2-foot by 10-foot blue and white vinyl banner hung on the front wall of our meeting room stating:

"TEC 192 Works on CEO Stuff."

It became their reminder to always be mindful of what their role is in their organization and what a true leader should be working and focusing on. Robert Halk reminds us that, "Delegating work works, provided the one delegating works, too."

In order to execute the fine art of delegation you must consider the following:

- What am I willing to let go of?
- Do I have anyone to hand off to?

Until you become clear on these two items I would stay put. Scrub your list of the activities that you do on a daily basis. Some of the tasks on your list are there because you like doing them. Others are there because you are best suited for them. A couple may still be on there because they are habitual and are part of the corporate wallpaper. Worst of all, some exist because you do not have the talent in your organization to download.

Refer back to the beginning of this chapter and match your daily activities to what I defined as the role of an effective leader of a small to midsize business. You know what is the right thing to do. You will have to spend some money. You will have to relinquish some control. You will have to let go of some of your pet tasks. You will have to move some people in and out of the organization. You will have to get out of your comfort zone. Just do it (thanks Nike).

Most importantly, you must assume the right and proper role in your business so that it may thrive and prosper. Remember, you deserve it.

I had Gary in my TEC Group for four years before I turned it over to my successor. He is still in the group and I hope he remains for years to come. Gary personified everything that I have discussed in this chapter. Gary earned his MBA from a prestigious Midwest university. He is a hired gun leading a business in the $150 million range, growing the business at 15 to 20 percent annually and producing profits that are approximately four to five times the industry average. He is a hot property and could run any business in any industry and be successful because he absolutely gets it.

I spent hundreds of hours with Gary picking his brain and exploring his success. Here is what I have discovered: He is the billboard for everything that we have discussed on leadership.

Gary realized that his people are the key to his own success. His next in command is better than Gary and he knew that when he hired him. He rejoices in making this decision. He has made certain that all his key reports have access to him at a personal and professional level. He spends a high percentage of his budget on training his people on the skills and behaviors that will move them and the business forward.

Gary is the most effective and intentional communicator I have ever encountered in the business world that I know. There is no ambiguity in his statements. The organization knows where it is going because Gary keeps it in their top-of-mind awareness. He is not embarrassed or shy about being redundant and repetitive.

Gary allows his direct reports to run their portion of the business, but when decisions are stalled or need to be accelerated, he takes full command. He makes few decisions, but the ones he makes are of high impact and courage.

There is no hiding the pea when is comes to this leader's principles. All who come into close contact with Gary clearly understand what he stands for. The organization is recognized as the leader in its market segment and Gary is nationally recognized for positions that he has taken in a tumultuous, bureaucratic and highly regulated industry. His strategies and decisions are always value-based so he sleeps soundly at night. His family comes first, business further on down the line. I would like for all of you to meet him. You would be better for it.

Review: To be a successful and effective leader of a small to midsize business you must:

1. Inspire, influence, and transform your people.
2. Set the corporate compass with your vision.
3. Be decisive.
4. Drive the business with *your* principles.
5. Delegate, then get busy doing what you are paid to do.

Robust actions to take:

1. Who in your organization do you need to spend more shoulder-to-shoulder time with developing their skills, behaviors, and leadership abilities?

2. When are you going to start your monthly one-to-ones with your direct reports?

3. Define your vision for your organization.

4. What decisions are you procrastinating on making?

5. What explicit principles do you want to make visible to your organization?

6. What tasks and responsibilities are you willing to delegate to another person in the organization?

Chapter Four

Strategy Four: Value Resiliency Over Brilliancy

Ya gotta do what ya gotta do.

—Sylvestor Stallone

Get over whatever "it" is fast.

As the leader of an organization facing unprecedented change and challenges, you do not have the luxury of throwing a prolonged pity party. You need to quickly work through adversity and get going again. You cannot go down with the Titanic. There are too many passengers and crewmembers depending on you to make the right move.

Get in the life raft, bark out some articulate, explicit orders, and start paddling. You are the shoulders that your company stands upon. You are the stuff that your company is made of. You are the person that others will turn to for guidance when the train has suddenly derailed. Unpleasant, unpredictable events are going to happen to you and your company in this post-modern business era. That is a given. Are you up to it?

You are not firewalled against misfortune. There are no moats between you and pending catastrophe. Key employees are going to leave, bankers are going to call loans, competitors are going to steal customers, governments are going to unfairly tax you, and occasionally you are going to have a miserable day with your nose flattened deep into an unforgiving and abrasive canvas mat. By the way, it hurts like hell!

Being off the charts smart, creative, innovative, a team player, a strategic thinker, a consensus builder is not going to get you through all of those moments. It may have got you an "A" in one of your business classes but that was years ago in a synthetic and unrealistic environment. Resilience is your hammer now. It is singularly your greatest strength. Use it and get up! Let me illustrate what resiliency means by examining the true-life business adventures of TEC members Emily and Derek.

Emily finished two years of college and went to work for a firm in a service business. She was bright, ambitious, and willing to work. She quickly learned what she needed to know and in her mid-twenties, along with a male partner, acquired the firm that had hired her and suddenly found herself an owner and CEO and beholding to the bank. The personal guarantees are something that most of you did not expect. She did not. Her ascension was fast and not quite anticipated. It was a meteoric rise; intellectually exhilarating, financially risky and kick started her on a journey as a leader of this and future organizations. Facing a slippery, vertical learning curve, she grew the business, made numerous rookie mistakes, survived through tenacity, hard work, and a little luck.

After a few years of difficulties, starts and stops, internal power struggles, circling, and competing in a rapidly and ever-changing business environment, the company settled into a predictable routine and made steady progress. Just when things were moving along smoothly the industry suffered a downturn, her male partner turned into a testosterone injected predator and Emily found herself on the short end of a naïve and ill conceived buy-sell agreement. She was young and inexperienced. Unexpectedly separated from the company that she helped grow and minus any sizeable return on investment, she deemed it all a good learning experience. Youth and unbridled optimism will do that for you.

Out on the corporate mean streets again with a scuffed up ego and an excellent reputation in her market, Emily was immediately recruited and hired by a regional leader in the industry and plopped in the president's seat of a high-profile major player. Back on her feet and upright. Vertical is good. She reported to the owner/CEO who now wanted to devote more time on another project and be freed from the day-to-day operations of the parent company. Emily was suddenly in the big leagues facing big league challenges and considering major league opportunities. She was wearing a new uniform but it felt a little tight in places.

Barely in her thirties she was neck deep in an extremely competitive market, working for a demanding and highly recognized CEO, fighting an organizational structure that had the owner's custom stamp deeply branded on it, facing employees who were unconditionally loyal to the former leader and dedicated to maintaining the status quo. Would you have taken this on?

Emily had challenges in both her professional and personal life. As the business demanded her focus and energy, her marriage began suffering from neglect and prickly unresolved issues. She was working deep into the dinner hour to put her imprint on the organization and trying like hell in whatever time was left in her day to salvage a teetering relationship.

Unbeknownst to others Emily was also at war with a substance abuse condition. She was drinking far too much, much too long, and entirely too often. Chardonnay had quietly and persistently captured more of her waking hours than ever before. She was functional but suspected that she was headed for trouble. She was. She is bright. She is conscious. Emily rationalized that her position as the designated leader of a prospering, well recognized organization demanded that she entertain existing customers and prospects, that she have a presence at citywide social events and be available at the drop of a hat for post-work gatherings with her new staff in order to bond with them. It seemed reasonable to her from her presidential swivel leather chair. All of these occasions involved drinking and her alcohol consumption continued to rise. It seemed manageable, but in reality, it was taking a toll on her energy, self-esteem, and spiritual life.

Faced with running a challenging business, returning home in the late evening to a faltering marriage, and experiencing a frustrating and an accelerating alcohol use, Emily had to regain control of her life and immediately extinguish her self-inflicted brush fires. Life, she was beginning to learn, is about choices and consequences. We read that in self-help books but seldom does it hit the sweet spot until it happens to us and suddenly we get it.

She went to work with intent, conviction, and renewed energy. On the job, Emily did the best that she could with what she had at her disposal and what she could internally control. The owner struggled with letting go and efforts that Emily made to move the organization toward her were consciously and unconsciously sabotaged or subtly put on the back burner by the CEO. In spite of the tacks in the road spread before her, over time she won the hearts, souls and minds of her inherited and newly hired employees, terminated the weak and nay-sayers, established firm financial controls, set a clear and passionate vision, opened new markets, grew the business in both revenue and profits, and performed commendably. Her scorecard was in the black.

While all this was taking place on the business front she and her husband were attending counseling sessions to determine whether or not they could salvage what they had in their relationship and build from that foundation into the future. It was taking an emotional toll on both parties. If that was not enough, Emily voluntarily enrolled in an outpatient alcohol rehabilitation program that demanded that she meet in group therapy sessions two times a week from 7 p.m. to 10 p.m., 30 miles from her office for the next six months. I am on overload just writing about it. She never missed a day at work; never skipped a counseling session with her husband, and her attendance in the rehabilitation program was perfect.

That was the good news. The rest of the news was that eventually she was unsuccessful in keeping the owner out of Emily's stable and was slowly but consistently losing her reins on the company that she was hired to lead. Recognizing the bold print handwriting being chiseled on the corporate wall and recognizing her inevitable fate Emily gracefully resigned leaving the organization better than when she was hired. It was a difficult and in her thinking a one-step-backward decision. The counseling sessions with her husband led to a painful but mutual decision to dissolve the marriage and to go their separate ways. Emily completed the six-month alcohol rehabilitation program, joined a professional woman's AA group, and has remained clean and sober now going on her fourth year.

No job, lost marriage, a lack of an alcohol escape mechanism, up off the mat she rose, a little bruised, a bit battered, but armed with her integrity, intelligence, resilience, and an expanded wisdom. Emily agreed with Harrison Ford the actor who said, "I realized early on that success was tied to not giving up. Most people in this business gave up and went on to other things. If you simply didn't give up, you would outlast the people who came in on the bus with you."

She immediately reset, wrote a business plan for a venture in a field new to her, furthered her education and due diligence by attending international workshops on the industry, and launched her infant company. That is being resilient, my friends, and it was a privilege to be at her side.

Resiliency is your differentiator. Leverage it.

Daniel Goleman in his book *Emotional Intelligence* states, "One source of a positive or negative outlook may well be an inborn temperament; some people by nature tend one way or the other. But, as we shall also see . . . temperament can be tempered by experience. Optimism and hope . . . like helplessness and despair . . . can be learned. Underlying both is an outlook psychologists call self-efficacy, the belief that one has mastery over the events of one's life and can meet challenges as they come up. Developing a competency of any kind strengthens the sense of self-efficacy, making a person more willing to take risks and seek out more demanding challenges. And surmounting those challenges in turn increases the sense of self-efficacy."

Stanford psychologist Albert Bandura further states that, "People who have a sense of self-efficacy bounce back from failure; they approach things in terms of how to handle them rather than worrying about what can go wrong." Kathleen Noble, Ph.D., in an article called *"Gifted Women: Identity and Expression"* wrote, "Resilience is a tri-fold process of recognizing and resisting the intrinsic and extrinsic obstacles that inhibit the development of one's potential . . . the way you go about enhancing resilience is to first of all recognize how critical a psychological factor it is."

My experience with successful leaders of small to midsize companies is that not only do they have the ability to tap into a high percentage of their human potential, in addition they have an abundance of self-efficacy that springs from both the inherent and experience well. Regardless of its source, it is a deeply embedded component of their inventory and a robust tool to leverage that provides them an extraordinary advantage over their competitors. They seldom back off when situations are not going their way. While others are licking their wounds and feeling sorry for their latest plight in life, the winners seize the opportunity to capitalize on other leader's prolonged recovery periods. They are up off the mat and moving forward to the center of the ring where the action takes place.

Remember you do not have a team of professional handlers (the MBAs) in your corner, applying wound healing ointment, snapping open smelling salts, and giving you a swig of mountain fresh spring water. You are there sitting on a corner stool basically all alone, facing the turbulence and wiping off your own eight-ounce padded gloves. The referee is going to call you to the center of the ring and the fight is going to continue for many more rounds. Are you up to it? Are you going to answer the bell? It is a choice.

Therefore, it does not matter if you were born with resilience or you acquired it while leaning back against the ropes doing your version of the Ali "rope-a-dope." If you want to be successful in leading a small to midsize business, it had better be a part of your repertoire. Got it?

Derek had created a holding company of six operating units threaded together by a loosely defined common interest.

He had hired or retained professional managers to run the individual businesses, consolidated accounting and other administrative operations and empowered his managers to make decisions and operate independently. His control was distant, non-invasive and in retrospect too hands off. He totally trusted his managers to keep him informed on the health of the businesses through his COO and involve him only in major decisions. At the time, it seemed like the right concept. It almost brought him down.

Unbeknownst to Derek, the COO of the holding company withheld information from Derek for ego purposes, control needs and a lack of his own "off the resume" talent. One dark and stormy day in Derek's life, it almost came apart. A prominent unit was in trouble, hemorrhaging cash, over-inventoried and poorly managed. It had been going on for some time and shielded from Derek's view. Derek had allowed his businesses to be leveraged too far, stretched too thin and controlled by others. The troubled company was putting at risk the remaining units along with Derek's net worth. Derek admittedly had considerable accountability in this unfortunate potential outcome. Do not we all? Ah, the webs we weave.

Keeping in mind that the darkest hour is only 60 minutes long, he stepped into the skirmish and took command. For Derek the challenges were both exhausting and unexpectedly exhilarating. Immediately he fired his COO. Derek felt betrayed. Over the next year he sold off the assets of the troubled company, renegotiated his financial situation with his bank that had changed hands several times, hired a new CFO, and grabbed possession of his cash flow. On the road, he consistently visited the five remaining operating companies, resetting their plans and establishing unfiltered communication lines between the operating managers and him.

In his early sixties, slightly overweight, quadruple bypass scars crisscrossing his chest, Derek put in long days and nights on the road and at the office. He was meeting with lawyers, customers, accountants, advisors, bankers and dealing with the day-to-day and long range stress of keeping the businesses intact and preventing his relatively small financial empire from collapsing. At times, his wife, the TEC group and I worried about his physical and mental health and wondered was it worth the pain and aggravation. He obviously thought it was and with determination plowed on.

His TEC Group advised him on numerous occasions to put the businesses on the market, pay off the remaining debt, and get on with his life. That was a reasonable solution and according to most everyone's opinion would eventually work. The numbers worked out. There would be ample capital left over after the debt was retired to do whatever he wanted to do. No way, declared Derek! He had fallen in love with the old Japanese proverb that stated, "Fall seven times, stand up eight." He stayed vertical. At times, he looked and felt like those inflatable bottom-weighted clown punching bags that once socked keeps popping back up daring you to take another punch. He never stayed down for very long.

Eventually he righted the businesses, stayed at the helm, and is now in the process of re-evaluating where he wants to go and what he wants to do with his life. Derek did his best to keep events and issues in perspective. Like best-selling author Robert Fulghum suggests, "If you break your neck, if you have nothing to eat, if your house is on fire, then you got a problem. Everything else is inconvenience."

You are going to make mistakes. That is a guaranteed reality. If you do not think you are going to blow it now and then, you are either an incredible genius immune to human frailties or in absolute denial. What if you are both? Resiliency is what is going to pull you through to the finish line. A little smarts also goes a long way.

Download resilience into your organization.

You might be resilient, but how do you get the organization to go there with you? Besides acting quickly and using resilience as your primary tool, I am going to share with you the strategies and actions I observed leaders and organizations implement when faced with difficult times and seemingly insurmountable challenges. You might be next, so sit up and pay good attention.

Most successful business leaders are able to:

- Make their personal resiliency unmistakably visible.
- Create a strong support group around them.
- Be willing to do something different.
- Throw intelligent and appropriate resources at the obstacle.

Make your personal resiliency unmistakably visible.

In working with business leaders of small to midsize organizations, I have concluded that for the most part organizations mirror the characteristics of the leader. So go you, so goes your business. I do not believe that opposites attract as much as I believe that people like to be around others just like them. Remember being "aware and beware" of the fishbowl? Your employees are watching you from sunrise to vespers and among many other things are trying to emulate your positive behavior, at least the keepers are. You have a running start at creating a resilient organization just by being highly visible day in and day out. Make bold moves in full view of your organization. Take responsibility, make what you do evident and see how much resiliency you can rub off on your organization. It is like super glue.

In a May 2002 *HBR* article entitled *How Resiliency Works* written by Diane Coutu, she says, "Resilient people . . . possess three characteristics; a staunch acceptance of reality, a deep belief, often buttressed by strongly held values, that life is meaningful; and an uncanny ability to improvise. You can bounce back from hardship with just one or two of these qualities, but you will only be truly resilient with all three. These three characteristics hold true for resilient organizations as well." Without question, the resilient leaders I worked with had an abundance of these three qualities.

One of the first CEOs to enroll in my TEC Group was Sid. He is a large, orangutan-like man with an enormous heart, laugh, and outlook on life. One of his favorite sayings is, "It just ain't no big deal." He is able to look at life that way because he searches for the truth in all situations instead of escaping to the safety net of denial, fantasy, opinion, and self-delusion. He understood that the truth is much easier to deal with than denial and fantasy. It is upright and ultimately undeniable. Challenges are not big deals to Sid because he approaches each one with a reality based humor, unwavering optimism, and resolve. Sid is a scientist by education, a business owner by choice and an incredible free spirit by incarnation.

Every February Sid and his wife travel to the Big Island of Hawaii, rent various types of lodging and settle in for 30 frolicking days away from the business. It is how Sid takes care of himself. Variety is essential for this particular business leader, so each year he chooses a skill or an expertise to become proficient at and that is his focus for one month. One year he learned how to weave baskets; another time he invented and manufactured non-alcoholic liquors; a recent vacation found him researching and devising a treatment program for his wife who had been diagnosed with breast cancer. It was always interesting to me and to his fellow TEC members to discover what the latest project was.

Month after month every TEC meeting starts with what we term an inclusion exercise where each member can update his colleagues on significant professional and personal activities of the previous month. It is a way of connecting after being separated for 30 days. As the roundtable discussion progressed it was Sid's turn.

"Well, let's see," Sid began looking down at the list he had prepared as prompts. "In February Joan and I took our annual trek to Hawaii. While there, I learned how to play the harp. Very difficult instrument to play, I might add. The business ran fantastic in spite of me not being there. In fact we had a record month. I just might stay away much longer next year. Let's see. Oh, while we were gone our waterfront house burned down to the ground destroying everything that we had leaving only a smoldering motor block in what used to be the garage. Everything was up in smoke. Our grand kids . . ."

"Err, ah . . . hold on just a minute Sid," I interrupted. "Did you just say you lost your house and all your life's possessions and it burned to the ground while you were on vacation?"

Sid surprisingly looked up from his list and said, "Yeah, but it just ain't no big deal. It happened the first week but there was no need to come back. Hell, nothing was left so what was the point? Besides, I was just starting to get the hang of that bloody harp. You know it was time to get some new stuff in our lives anyway, never was that crazy about the house (big hearty laugh), and I figured it was just the Universe's way of telling me to stop being so complacent and to get going again. We have plenty of insurance so it will all work out fine." We all leaned forward in our chairs slightly stunned at what we had just heard. Most of us were thinking, "How can he be so lighthearted over what most families would consider an absolute tragedy? What about the family pictures?"

That is vintage Sid. He keeps events in perspective, tries to see the good that might come out of an incident, and realizes that the only outcome he can control is his reaction to what is happening. He takes the high road; eyeball-to-eyeball he stares reality down and gets creatively busy. Sid sees the bigger picture and realizes that no real harm was done because no lives were lost or endangered. He keeps life's circumstances inside parameters so that he can effectively deal with them. Everything that had been destroyed could be replaced in some fashion, even upgraded. His spiritual foundation allows him and Joan to look at the event as an opportunity for new beginnings, fresh adventures, and letting go of the past.

Six months later, Sid was enjoying a new single-story home on a different low bank waterfront lot, a cactus-inspired Southwest interior décor, and current family photographs perched throughout the home, Joan's cancer in remission, and the latest wardrobe for him and his wife. Life and "it" just continues to go on.

Like Diane Coutu suggests, resiliency is about being real, looking for meaning in circumstances, and doing what you have to do in innovative ways. The TEC Group observed our colleague; Sid's employees watched their leader, and we learned firsthand in real time what resiliency looks like and is all about.

Create a strong support group around you.

Resilient people do not do it all alone. They have figured out that they can only stretch themselves so far before they eventually unravel. When unexpected challenges knock on your door, call in the team and even the odds with whatever you are facing. This is not the time for taking "macha and macho" stances in life. Rally the troops!

In an afternoon session in a TEC meeting a few years back, a shaken veteran member brought up the following issue for us to advise him on. Dan was a local manufacturer in the perishable food industry. His products were well branded, gourmet quality, and sold well at both local and regional grocery retail outlets. Unfortunately, Dan discovered that he was just dropped by a major customer after a long-term seemingly healthy relationship. Overnight, without any overt warning, he lost 25% of his business. It had vanished. That hurts. When you own a small business something like that gets your attention and tends to spoil your day.

The group worked on the issue for the remainder of the meeting. Dan admitted that perhaps he had gotten a bit complacent, lost contact with the account as food brokers represented his products, and he was not paying as much attention to his revenue stream as he had in the past. Comfort and familiarity had crept in. He had dozed off. The conversation with the group revealed that the loss of the account was not about price, service, sales, quality or anything that we could get a stranglehold on. All Dan knew was that he was losing his slot on their shelves along with considerable sales and profits.

The group suggested a multitude of strategies, discussed contingencies, and before the day was over, Dan walked out of the meeting with a well thought out streamlined game plan on how he was going to weather the financial turbulence and regain the account. The group helped him to "chunk down" the problem and focus on two vital and essential outcomes. It kept him from being overwhelmed and diluting his resilience. It was a start and there would be many revisions as the conversation continued. A renewed bounce in Dan's step propelled him out the meeting door as we adjourned the session. He got the help he needed and was not facing this alone.

Since Dan admitted to becoming a bit lackadaisical in his leadership, one of the mandates of the group was that whatever he decided to do, he had to answer to the members on an ongoing basis. We wanted to be kept up to date on his activities, tactics, and movement. Not only were we going to hold his feet to the fire on implementation, but we were also going to be there for him emotionally, spiritually, and physically as much as possible as he faced the daunting task of winning back the mega account and staying above his financial waterline. TEC has allowed business leaders to realize that "lonely at the top" is an archaic notion and a poorly conceived choice. We were not going to let Dan go down on our watch.

War was declared and Dan led the troops but not too far out in front. He kept his employees well informed of what was happening. They had strategy, brainstorming and small town hall meetings to dispel rumors and eliminate obstacles that might surface. A group of advisors were formed separate from his TEC Group to give him an additional objective perspective. This team was populated with accountants, lawyers, vendors, and other professional people in his industry. Dan surrounded himself with people that could assist him in moving through this setback. He rallied loyal customers and met with them to see what could be done. He had his advisory support teams in place to assist him in meeting the challenges ahead and to boost his confidence.

Be willing to do something different.

Dan's objectives were to stay financially healthy and get back on the shelves of the regional grocery chain. Being resilient does not mean being stubborn and keep firing the same shells at the same target. That approach is more like being persistent. New approaches had to be considered and implemented. Over the years, Dan had sold his products through food brokers or with in-house sales people. For years, it had been a successful approach. That was then but this is now. The food brokers had been calling on the buyer in that particular department and making no progress. They were being stonewalled and could not penetrate the account through the traditional existing channel. Dan decided to become the primary contact man with the account and returned to an earlier strategy that he implemented when building the business. He became the Chief Sales Officer. Through his reputation, position and relationships he was able to meet with the leader of the lost account. The meetings were cordial but non-committal. Dan did not learn anything new or gain much headway but respected the leader's decision to let his buyers run their segment of the business. Doors were kept open and Dan had to try a different, more effective strategy.

With his financial well-being and net worth on the line, Dan kept plugging away with the resources he had available. He kept respectful communications lines open to the leadership, managed his cash the best that he could and kept pursuing new business. While all of this was taking place a groundswell of customers was building up on the shores of the retailer wondering where their favorite product was and what was this other product doing on the shelf? The specific department was bombarded with questions, concerns, and requests that the product be returned. Some customers threatened to take their business to competitors. Articles appeared in industry publications and local newspapers about the sudden and mysterious disappearance of Dan's products. What was occurring was a pull through strategy in forward gear and working better than anticipated.

After approximately one year of major account drought Dan had a surprise visit from one of the leaders of his former customer. He asked that Dan come back, reclaim his slots, and let what had happened in the past be long gone. They started over and business was restored. He had simply stayed on the bus.

Throw intelligent and appropriate resource at the obstacle.

When faced with company-threatening adversity there is no reason to hold back resources. Let us review what Dan set in motion to overcome this setback.

Dan:

- Became absolutely real about the situation and recognized the immediate impact it had on his business's cash flow and his personal net worth.
- Got help and did not allow himself to be isolated in facing the difficulty.
- Established an accountability relationship with his peers.
- Kept respectful communications lines open to all concerned.
- Personally got involved and invested in solving the problem.
- Kept it simple and focused on two primary objectives.
- Called in some chits.
- Did not burn bridges.
- Tried something new.
- Hung in there and stayed on the bus!

You will have your own version of this. I am not suggesting that this is the absolute, hands-down guaranteed model for working through business speed bumps, but it worked for Dan and is a possible template for you regarding whatever you are facing. I believe that good businesses get better in bad times and bad businesses no longer record a recognizable blip. Good businesses get better because their leaders keep them from disappearing into the La Brea tar pits of dinosaur companies by remaining resilient and teaching their organizations to be likewise. Dan attacked this problem from a variety of fronts keeping actions and strategies simple, straightforward, and concentrating his limited resources on two specific outcomes . . . profitability and regaining the account.

I have never been a complete fan of the David and Goliath one sling, one rock strategy. I want low cost options in my arsenal launching from multiple strategic positions. Optimism and resiliency suggests that somewhere under all that horse crap there is a pony in there.

I believe that this resiliency characteristic is your trump card. Play it for all it is worth. Stay on the bus, keep looking through the windshield, and resist the temptation to follow the crowd and flood the exit doors as soon as "it" gets a little testy. Resilience has gotten you to where you are now and it still has a long and productive shelf life.

Review: To be a successful and effective leader of a small to midsize business you must:

1. Get over whatever "it" is fast.
2. Understand that resiliency is your differentiator. Leverage it.
3. Download resilience into your organization.
4. Make your personal resiliency unmistakably visible.
5. Create a strong support group around you.
6. Be willing to do something different.
7. Throw intelligent and appropriate resource at the obstacle.

Robust actions to take:

1. Currently what is the most challenging "it" in your business?

2. What are you doing about it?

3. If you were to create an advisory group, how would you use them?

4. Who specifically would you choose?

5. What is your plan to create resiliency in your company?

Chapter Five

STRATEGY FIVE: IT'S ALL ABOUT THE PEOPLE

I get satisfaction of three kinds.
One is creating something.
One is being paid for it. And
one is the feeling that I haven't been
sitting on my ass all afternoon.

—William F. Buckley

Extraordinary people create consistent, extraordinary results.

Few business leaders of small to midsize companies seldom experience an outstanding corporate result in spite of their employees. The ultimate success in any business depends upon the quality of the human currency working in lockstep within the walls of the organization and by placing the right butts in the right seats at the right time. A great plan, strategy, vision, or clever and brilliant leadership seldom survives its ultimate head-on collision with a low DNA factor. That intersection is filled with mangled strategic plans, loss of bottom line profits, frustration, and wasted, unproductive time.

I will admit that during certain critical circumstances seemingly ordinary people rise to the occasion to produce unbelievable and unanticipated outcomes. Every once in a while, the cover is knocked off the ball. Specific emergency events often prove that extraordinary performance is possible. However, if I am sitting in the corner office of my business, I do not want to wait for the adrenaline to start surging through direct report veins and the sirens to start wailing before my selected team rises to the occasion and bails the business and my net worth out of harm's way. I demand daily, consistent, predictable high performance, and I assure you it is not going to come from dull steak knives in your corporate drawer or elevators that do not go all the way to the presidential penthouse suite.

I am not telling you anything you do not know. It is just once in awhile you suffer from an unanticipated acute amnesia attack and try to do what you do completely alone or with limited human resources, and then sit back in wonderment and disbelief observing that the project failed or imploded on the launch pad. It is good to have rocket scientists on your team during design, lift-off, orbit, and re-entry.

You know what the problem is; the most talented people in the available employee marketplace are not lined up outside your Human Resources Director's door, if you even have one, begging to go to work for you. There are good productive people queuing up seeking employment and opportunity with your organization, but not the same caliber crowd FedExing résumés to Fortune 500 companies and to the other behemoth competitive players roaming the globe. You usually attract and ultimately hire second and third-tier talent. That is a fact regarding small to midsize businesses.

There is a way to increase your odds of attracting and hiring extraordinary talent. I am going to share with you what I have observed your most successful colleagues do to boost their talent pool and give themselves a competitive edge.

Make it the priority.

It is essential that your number-one priority in your business be the intentional and proactive:

- recruitment
- hiring
- training
- and retention

of the best talent available. It is not always easy but it is always essential. Most companies of your size approach these personnel tasks on a 911 basis. When the need raises its ugly head you become instantly active and frantically start the game of catch up. Under those circumstances, it is too late and not very effective. Get in front of this issue and strategically approach this matter as if it were of utmost importance. It is. Try implementing strategies, completing tasks, reaching goals, being creative, and building your net worth with minimum and questionable talent. That is a formula guaranteeing disappointment and chronic leadership heartburn.

When I facilitate strategic planning sessions with companies, I insist that the number-one priority be securing and retaining extraordinary talent. It is a good business strategy because I can be somewhat confident that the plan that I assist in creating for the organization has a good chance of being implemented and assuring ongoing future business with that client.

Systemize this process. Make your system dealing with talent highly visible, well thought out, thoroughly understood and consistent in the organization. Keep evaluating what is working and what needs tweaking, or a major up-on-the-hydraulic lift overhaul. Do not fall asleep when it comes to your people. You have spent countless hours and invested considerable dollars in creating systems and processes for manufacturing, invoicing, collecting receivables, sales management and all other functions of your business. Most of you approach the people issue with malignant casualness and benign neglect. It deserves better. I know that some of you believe that if it were not for all those damn people around your plant you just might get something done. That dictates an immediate attitude adjustment. People are not going to go away, so figure out how you can deliberately and strategically approach and maximize your return on this essential resource. You must become an expert in understanding human beings. Good luck!

A B R: Always be recruiting.

This should be the mantra of your Human Resources Director. Good chance you do not have one down the hall, but if you happen to and they have a wide band skill level, elevate this function in your company from compliance, benefit packages, and touchy-feely personal counseling to being the VIP in charge of procuring talent. It is not enough for the Human Resources VP to keep the cafeteria "sue the company for free" bulletin board bombarded with all the latest threats and edicts from the government and labor unions or to devote their activities to fulfilling the role of mother-father confessor. I just hate that when it happens. This job is and should be more all-inclusive. It is your direct channel to extraordinary talent. That should be the number-one objective and primary focus of your Human Resources person. Why settle?

If you do not have an internal Human Resources function in your business then outsource it to a contract firm who specializes in all the extended and inclusive activities of a true professional in Human Resources. Do not drop it on your controller's or CFO's shoulders. Remember, for the most part, people and their nagging petty issues are irritating to financial types. Consultants in this field have informed me that the magic number is 100 employees, and at that point Human Resources comes in-house along with a hefty salary plus comprehensive benefits. Do what works for you, but in any case, redirect your entire work force into HR advocates, and all of you participate in implementing **ABR**. You must lead the charge.

Keep a talent file handy. Consistently fill that folder with the business cards and résumés of talented people who you and your employees encounter in your world. If the person selling you a new cell phone makes a favorable impression on you, ask for their card and have a brief conversation with them relative to your company and opportunities that exist for them. Develop a well-rehearsed, articulate, compelling and convincing stump/elevator speech. Keep in touch. All of your managers should do the same so you have an active and current inventory of prospects to **ABR**.

Be imaginative while bringing your best and brightest people periodically together to create and implement strategies to increase the talent quotient in your business. You do this when considering other business matters. Why not with people? Remember, winners like to be with other winners but not necessarily in the same department. Not necessarily on the same horizontal line on your organization chart competing for the next slot on the company's food chain or capturing that outstanding performance bonus.

Please understand that there is one inherent and predictable problem. You are the only person in your enterprise who will aggressively and deliberately hire someone better than you. Your direct reports will swear on the Bible, the Koran, while saluting the American flag, that what I just suggested is not even close to the truth; that they would have no issue, whatsoever, with personally recruiting and hiring a person that is smarter, more talented, better dressed, more handsome/beautiful, with skill sets far beyond their own. Do not fall for that one. Watch their nose for immediate "prolongation." No one is deliberately going to create terminal obsolescence for him or herself. You need to be the lead dog. It is the best view.

Hire fast, fire faster.

Put considerable thought in how your organization is approaching the issue of hiring extraordinary talent. At one time, I bought into the popular notion of "hire slow, fire fast." That was a good and logical sound bite when the velocity of change in the business world was just chugging predictably along. You, as the leader, had the luxury of thoroughly investigating whether or not a certain potential employee was going to be a decent fit with your organization. There was ample time to contemplate, interrogate, investigate, integrate, propagate, and implement all the other "ates" before making a decision on any specific candidate. This approach does not work as well now as it did in the recent past. You still need to do all the "ates" but you need to do them more quickly, with more intensity and with more intention.

Hire fast, fire even faster is now more appropriate. It is a prerequisite that you have a streamlined, well thought out procedure that accelerates the decision-making process regarding people coming and going. If you or your direct reports are snail slow in making decisions on hiring talented and terminating untalented people, you are going to come in second place. First place is more fun. The ribbon is blue and flashbulbs are popping.

In this free agent environment, the winners have more options and an abundance of suitors more so than ever before. Top organizations have figured out how to move people quickly through to decision intersections, keep them tethered to the mother ship and to get them on board.

Here is what you need to do. Investigate and select a suitable testing instrument that provides you a penetrating and revealing look inside the person you are interviewing. Go deep. Remember from a previous chapter that people walk into your organization with their own embedded behavioral software and you had better make certain that it is compatible with the cultural and behavioral software in your organization. You are not and never should be in the behavior modification business. It is not your expertise. How successful have you been doing this with your teenage daughters and sons? Besides, you love them, they love you, and you still cannot get it done. Give it up and hire people who demonstrate the qualities that you desire inside the walls of your business. Test for it.

Design and implement a consistent, repetitive, and effective, interviewing methodology. Invest in training your existing employees on how they can effectively and efficiently evaluate prospective candidates. A cynical part of me believes that hiring is a crapshoot regardless of what you do, but let us put some deliberate thought into this most important function and do the best that we can to place the odds in your favor.

There is an art and science in productive interviewing and you need to investigate and decide what allows you the best chance in determining who you are bringing into your organization. Remember that once in they are difficult and expensive to extract.

I have observed firsthand ineffective interviewing. Here is how it usually goes.

Interviewer, "We here at Acme Manufacturing believe that teamwork is an essential ingredient in our success. Tell me, do you believe that teamwork is essential?"

Prospect, "I believe it is the only way to be successful in any organization."

Well, excuse me. The candidate would have to be a world-class, out-of-the-box blithering moron or an unemployed relative to answer that question in any other way. Like I said before, the past is the best predictor of the future, and the interviewer should have said, "We at Acme Manufacturing believe that the cornerstone to our success is teamwork. You have an impressive resume and certainly possess the skill sets that we are looking for. Please share with me a time that you were on a high-performing team at your previous job; what was the team all about, what did you accomplish, and what was your contribution? I would also appreciate, if you would (compliance issue), the names of your teammates, their telephone numbers, and e-mail addresses. Take your time . . . this is important."

I will ask and I will check if given permission. I demand compatible software. Put the odds in your favor.

Tomorrow I am going to have someone else in the company interview this candidate and ask the same questions. Afterwards we are going to huddle and compare notes. The truth is easy to remember and lies are very often difficult to consistently recall.

Be willing to open up your pocketbook a bit wider and deeper to pay for talent. Like everything else in life, you usually get what you pay for. Do not be a tightwad. I was having a one-to-one with a TEC member (Mike), and before we started, he had to show me the new machine he purchased to increase productivity and streamline production. Out into the manufacturing floor we rushed. He was full of vim and vigor, enthusiasm and passion, excitement and confidence. I found myself standing before a $3 million, computer-driven, high-speed gizmo that was guaranteed to increase productivity, reduce expenses and deliver at a speed never before imagined. The CEO did not have a clue to how this marvel of modern technology actually worked, but he bought into its benefits and agreed to pay the asking price. As we were walking back to his office, we passed the littered cubicle of Frank the bookkeeper who was methodically preparing the monthly profit and loss statement counting revenue and expenses on his fingers and toes. Mike was full of resignation, passivity, and disinterest. Frank only cost this member a visible $40,000 a year in salary, but I wondered how much the real price was?

The CEO considered his bookkeeper a financial bargain, but was he really? Many of our one-to-one conversations centered upon Frank as his financial reports were chronically late, he wasn't much of a team player, he seemed preoccupied in detail and never really participated in shaping the company's strategy. In addition, he seldom worked with the banks, passing off that responsibility to the owner, and he was not up on the latest financial management software, but he was cheap, familiar, and had been there a long time.

I question what keeps leaders from investing in people at the same scale and confidence that they invest in tangible assets. Where do you stand in this decision? What do you value the most? What prices are you paying for discounting the contribution of your people to your success? What are you willing to pay for extraordinary talent and peace of mind?

Train to retain your winners.

Effective training, challenging assignments and retention of your best people go hand in hand. Pay close attention. It costs employers 50% to 150% of an existing employee's annual fully loaded salary to hire their replacement. Search efforts, training costs, loss of productivity and stalling momentum escalate the expense of losing key people. You must become focused on doing something about this extremely costly and company-threatening condition. Keep your game breakers.

Winners currently view themselves as free agents, owners, and investors. That is an unprecedented mindset. It is a new ball game with new rules and requires a different approach by leadership (that's you).

Being *free agents* the 30-year gold watch loyalty scheme is history from both the employer and employee standpoint. The loyalty relationship between employee and employer has diminished from both sides. Highly talented people are more mobile, more willing to seek and respond to opportunity, and more visible in the marketplace than ever before. Thank the digital world and the information age for that. You are fortunate if you can corral talent for four to five years before they move on to a more enticing offer or initiate their own startup or acquisition.

As *owners* they demand the opportunity for personal and professional growth to increase their personal inventory of skills, wisdom and knowledge, which they carry within them wherever they eventually land. That is where a comprehensive training program and challenging assignments come into play.

Seeing themselves as *investors* they realize that the more they own, grow, learn and expand their skill, knowledge and leadership abilities, the more valuable they become in the marketplace as investors seeking a high return on investment for what they bring to the corporate conference table. My mentor, Jim Jensen, suggests that your goal as an employer is to assist your employees to become better all-around people not necessarily just better employees. They just might recognize that this is important and spend a few more years with you. Remember "balance"?

Enter into the conversation with your key people. Stay current with the folks who are making you successful. Do not be held hostage by them by trying to satisfy unreasonable and selfish demands but do determine what it will take to Velcro them to your organization for as long as possible. Regardless of what you hear them say or watch them do, they are ultimately tuned in to an FM station with the call letters W. I. I. F. M. broadcasting live from deep within their own personal needs and considering the question "what's in it for me?" You will need to negotiate to a "win-win" end-result on that question.

You should never be surprised or caught off guard by the sudden and unexpected departure of one of your winners if you have engaged with them in a candid and ongoing developmental dialogue. Keep the conversation current.

Get rid of deadwood now.

This gets a bit tricky for a couple of reasons. First, not many people enjoy waking up in the morning knowing that what they must do that day is terminate an employee or two, and second, the primary strategy of deadwood is to stay off the corporate radar screen and be difficult to detect. Get over the first one and know the second tactic does not work that well. People are known by the company they keep, and companies are known by the people they keep. Who are you keeping that you should not be? What is it costing you? How does this reflect on your business and you as the leader?

I want to make one thing very clear. I am not a "chainsaw" fan. I believe it is right, fair, and proper to give people every opportunity to succeed. You must provide the resources, mentoring, clear expectations, and support they need to accomplish their objectives. Make certain you have them in the right seats doing what they do best. Foster an attitude of wanting your employees to do well and then do what is necessary, within reason, to assist them in reaching that outcome. When they demonstrate to you that they are incapable or unwilling to step up and/or display behavior that is unacceptable to you, then it is time to turn them loose and for you to get some well-deserved sleep.

Keep in mind that you must take every opportunity available to consistently upgrade the talent in your organization. Turn this seemingly stressful dismissal into a positive, proactive action and not a heavy negative burden. You are making the right decision even if you are tossing and turning all night and feel like throwing up.

I realize that going through the process of firing an employee is not an all-encompassing pleasant experience. The majority of you are nice people and "executing" an employee causes stress on your over-sensitive psyche. Get past it. Remember that at times it is easier and less stressful to change people than it is to change people.

As a speaker colleague Will Phillips says, "Value honesty over niceness." What is your niceness costing you and the organization? The honest approach is for you to confront the dilemma and promptly act within your value system. You are probably the only one losing sleep regarding this matter. It will not be as difficult as your imagination has projected. Why do most of you go to worst-case scenarios when it comes to people? The marginal, equity-eroding employee sleeps peacefully each night knowing that they have successfully stolen one more day on the job and eagerly accepted another "company welfare check" from you. Thank you very much! That is the truth and you all, at some level, know it. The day after you actually "make someone available to industry" as my friend, Horatio Alger Award winner Red Scott describes this activity, your door is filled with employees asking you why it took so long.

So why does it take you so long? What are your excuses

for jeopardizing and putting at risk your hard-fought net worth and financial security? Here are a few of the classic, imaginative excuses and unreasonable reasons I have heard:

- "I didn't notice it as I was busy doing other things."
  (denial strategy)
- "I thought it would work itself out."
  (divine intervention strategy)
- "It is their manager's responsibility not mine."
  (not accountable, pass the buck strategy)
- "The timing is not right."
  (procrastination strategy)
- "The devil I know is better than the devil I don't know."
  (head up your rump strategy)
- "But I know their family, in fact it is mine."
  (poor genetics and Catholic/Jewish guilt strategy)
- And many more
  (unlimited rationalization strategies)

I consulted for a brief period with a CEO of a small international public company that in my estimation lopped off people in a cruel and ineffective manner. Annually he and his numerous (maybe a control issue here) direct reports participated in a mandatory, two-day, off-site "slaughter." The drill consisted of subjectively evaluating their 100 employees one through 100 with no two employees occupying the same slot. Being number one was great; being number 90 through 100 had some vulnerability problems. The managers had to include themselves in the ranking while excluding the CEO. He was no dummy.

Immediately upon returning from the off-site meeting (Monday morning) the bottom 10 (90 through 100) would be summoned into their manager's office, handed a blindfold and a cigarette and told to have their desk emptied by the time the sun set that day. In full view of their relieved peers, a security guard would be escorting them out the door with cardboard box loaded with pictures of their children and other company memorabilia tucked under their arm. Security, the Human Resources Director, the payroll clerk, the bottom 10 employees, and their department managers had a very busy and extremely excruciating day.

Can you imagine the anxiety and turbulence that was created in the organization, as the management team pulled into the company parking lot after their "lost" and perhaps "last" weekend together? Is there any way to determine the cost associated with the loss of focus, productivity, and morale of this organization as the employees anticipated the retreat, waited for their score and the accompanying summons to see the hangman that Monday morning? Now there is a hell of a way to start your week.

Put yourself in the shoes of the Human Resources Director and the challenges of rapidly implementing mass terminations and replacing employees from all departments. Think about the liability and exposure to subsequent wrongful termination lawsuits, sexual and age discrimination complaints, and possible complications caused by a lack of documentation and personnel paper trails. The CEO was blind to all of this vulnerability and believed that this was a fantastic idea he obtained from one of Jack's books and a useful strategy to raise the level of performance and talent in his organization. Maybe it worked for Jack but it did not work so well for this "JW knockoff." While Jack moved on with his stock options, corporate jet, and New York apartment, our boy was left with paranoid employees, low-morale and an organization that failed to attract extraordinary people with high self-esteem. We parted company, as did many of his talented people. It was crowded at the exits. This is not a good model unless you have extraordinary talent lined up and pounding on your door. Do not do it.

Be compassionate when removing the deadwood, but extricate it. You either directly or indirectly hired and/or inherited them at one time so you have direct accountability in this issue. You also played a cameo role in their lack of success in conscious and unconscious ways. Again, get over it and please do not set them up for life with an overly generous severance package to soothe your guilt. This is not fun but it needs to be done. That last sentence rhymes and will make it easy to remember.

"Show and tell" them that you care.

"I literally trust you with my life. This business, that I created, is my life and if I didn't deeply care about each one of you of you in this room I would never consider relinquishing the control and power that I, ultimately used to have, to all of you. I am and have been over the years handing my fate over to you. You're the primary reason for my success. You know that, don't you?" Randy's eyes began to moisten as he spoke to his management team while concluding a two-day strategic planning retreat that I was facilitating. His voice was soft, his speech unexpectedly uneven, the message curiously unfamiliar.

This successful Owner/CEO was, for the first time in his 25-year career, explaining to his direct reports what they all meant to him and how important they all were to his life and peace of mind. Collective gulps and sighs could be heard from this highly attentive band of frontline managers.

He had been to their birthday parties, attended their weddings, occupied a front row seat at their first-born baptisms, and celebrated with them as they moved up the organization chart. Randy sponsored company picnics, hosted Christmas parties, and said hello to his staff as he walked the halls of his organization. He assumed that they must all be aware of his level of interest in them as individuals. He assumed that they all knew how much he trusted and cared for them. Surely, his actions spoke much louder than his lack of words. Assuming can be misleading. Now, as he was about to step out of the everyday leadership of the company that he founded, he made it official as to how much he valued the people who worked for him and contributed to his good fortune. His management team, perhaps for the first time, really got it. It was not too late but it was late.

Make it official early on in the game. Your people will crawl across the world on razor blades if they sense that you really do care for them. They need to know and you need to make it explicit. People want to know that others value and are concerned about them. Go far beyond the generally expected. It is sound business. Be genuine. This is not the time, nor the place, for empty, trite platitudes, and synthetic expressions of caring and concern. High-performance people have acute bullshit detectors, so be sincere.

When I was playing organized high school and intercollegiate sports many of my coaches would periodically ream me and my other teammates up one wall and down another for a performance that was not up to their established standards. We would be chastised, criticized, and humiliated both in private and in full review of our relieved colleagues. We called it being "ripped a new one." By the way, that really hurts emotionally and physically. Following the "feedback" episodes we were informed by the righteous coach that they certainly would not have behaved in that manner had they not cared for us so much. Right!

Be thoughtful and appropriate when expressing your care and concern for your employees. People process information according to their individual filters not yours. You want the message to be heard and fully understood, so you might have to customize your delivery depending upon the recipient and the situation.

Please make certain that you do the following:

- Spend scheduled quality one-on-one time with your keepers.
  Robust actions I will take:

- Give them continual developmental feedback, not punitive.
  Robust actions I will take:

- Challenge them with interesting, stretching, assignments and keep raising the bar.
  Robust actions I will take:

- Go out to a bar/restaurant (out with them) and pick up the tab.
  Robust actions I will take:

- Write them personal notes of congratulation (not e-mails).
  Robust actions I will take:

- Publicly and privately, acknowledge their outstanding performance.
  Robust actions I will take:

- Design a career path with them.
  Robust actions I will take:

- Coach, mentor, and role model.
  Robust actions I will take:

- Help them to align their goals with your business goals.
  Robust actions I will take:

- Criticize the performance not the performer.
  Robust actions I will take:

- Follow-up with them on agreed upon personal and professional outcomes.
  Robust actions I will take:

- Always be a trusted and enthusiastic advocate of their self-esteem.
  Robust actions I will take:

- Above all else, listen, listen, and listen.
  Robust actions I will take:

- And much more (start with how do you want to be cared for and valued?).
  Robust actions I will take:

I heard Dr. Phil tell his television audience that to show people that you really care for them you must challenge and support their efforts to be committed to do what they need to do to have what they want to have. That makes incredible sense. I want you to be in a professional relationship with a person playing that role in their life. Go do it.

Review: To be a successful and effective leader of a small to midsize business you must:

1. **Understand that consistent, extraordinary results are created by extraordinary people.**
2. **Make it the priority to proactively recruit, hire, train, and retain extraordinary talent.**
3. **Get rid of deadwood now.**

4. "Show and tell" them that you care.

Robust actions to take:

1. What are you going to do to raise the level of talent in your organization?

2. What do you need to do to be more proactive in recruiting, hiring, training, and retaining extraordinary talent?

3. What do you need to do to extricate the deadwood in your organization?

4. What are you going to do to express the care that you have for your employees?

Chapter Six

STRATEGY SIX: UNDERSTANDING YOUR NUMBERS IS NOT AN OPTION

Cash ain't cash unless it's cash.

—Red Scott

**You are in business to make money.
Get everyone's attention.**

I wish that I could pick up the current *Wall Street Journal*, turn to the financial section, scan the quarterly report on XYZ Corporation, and discover that my favorite company is a good and gracious community neighbor. In addition, they provide wonderful perks, comprehensive benefits for their employees, make substantial annual contributions to local charities, and so on. Unfortunately, what are reported are revenues, earnings, price-to-earnings ratios, market capitalization, and a multitude of other revealing, stark statistics. What I really wish that I could do is buy a *Wall Street Journal* one day in advance of its publication. A fellow could make some real money doing that.

I must remind you, and you must continually remind your employees, that the primary reason you are in business is to ethically and consistently make money. Lots of cash. Period. End of story! No other acceptable options come first. It is not about realizing your ultimate dream, continuing another generation of a family business, being independent, or anything else. All of those reasons are important and honorable, but you will not have an opportunity to experience any of them if you do not deliberately subordinate them to being financially vibrant. Everything else in your business comes in second place except your principles for they determine the manner in which you ultimately secure your profits.

The scorecard (your income, your cash flow statement, and your balance sheet) reports the statistics that indicate whether you and your employees are allowed to come to work the following morning. Remember what educator and writer Laurence J. Peter said? "Don't knock the rich. When did a poor person give you a job?" You can create and implement all that other feel-good stuff once the profits are secured and safely deposited in your corporate vault.

Keep this one thought in your top-of-mind awareness. It is your net worth and your equity that is always at risk. You need to focus on and create a consistent vertical ascension in profits and revenue to stay vigorous, active, and alive, in the game of being in a business. Gather, interpret, and understand what the numbers of your business are saying to you. They tend to shout loud and clear if you are listening and paying close attention. If you do not, you are surely lost and riding downhill rails to a very nasty train wreck with your net worth dangling from a narrow gauge railroad trestle. Below, the gorge is cold, ambivalent and does not give a hoot whether you succeed or fail.

Pound your financial stakes in terra firma.

Financial management is another system in your business. You need to treat it as such, and intentionally, consciously and deliberately decide how you want it to be. Do not make it up as you and your employees move along on your journey. If you are reading this book, there is a good chance that you have climbed up your bell shape curve past the "I don't know if I'm going to make it" stage. The experimenting should be over, and by this time, the financial approach to your business should be in the ever evolving, refining, tinkering phase, and no longer a dipping into the cigar box, start-up tactic.

What are your fiscal goals? How are you going to measure them? What systems do you need to install and implement to reach the identified financial objectives? What are you doing to educate yourself and your employees on sound monetary management? What is your budgeting process? How do you communicate the financial health of the organization to your employees, your bank, the other share and stakeholders? I have many more questions for you to consider but this is a good start. You still have orders to get out the door by this afternoon.

My most successful clients and TEC members were clear on the following:

- What the organization needed to do relative to its continuous financial health.
  Robust actions I will take:

- What percentage growth rate they wanted to grow the business.
  Robust actions I will take:

- What the industry financial standards were and how they matched up with their company's fiscal results.
  Robust actions I will take:

- What percentage of sales or actual dollars they established as goals for their various margin lines.
  Robust actions I will take:

- How much debt or cash was required to maintain or grow the business and at what interest rate.
  Robust actions I will take:

- How regularly and with what content did they want their financial reports to contain as they landed on their desks.
  Robust actions I will take:

- What they wanted defined in the budgets, how the process was implemented, and how people and departments were held accountable.

  Robust actions I will take:

- What they wanted the value of the company to be when it was time to take hard-earned chips off the table.

  Robust actions I will take:

Think through these questions and make them essential elements in your strategic and operational planning. Create strategies, goals, and actions that accelerate you and the organization toward the stakes. Hold those who are the implementers accountable for hitting the targets. Provide them adequate support so they might succeed. Establish consequences for those who continually come up short. Make visible the progress or lack of movement toward the goals. Implement immediate actions to correct the situation by declaring war on the obstacles. Keep current and exact score.

Create your box score.

When I was a kid, I scrutinized, studied, and memorized the box scores, standings, and statistics of my major league baseball heroes and teams. The numbers exposed and forecasted slumps, identified winning and losing streaks, showed who was hot and who was not, and among other things, predicted trends, recorded results and suggested future outcomes. You need, with the same enthusiasm and devoted interest of a young, fanatic, baseball nut, to do the same with your company's box score. If you fail to do this, you might be in for a long season characterized by mounting losses, strikeouts, bean balls, and disgruntled, fickle fans that take no pleasure being down in the cellar with you.

What are your corporate equivalents of at bats, hits, runs, errors, strikeouts, and walks that tell the story about your day, week, month, and year at the office? Do you have a process that indicates to you in a timely and concise manner the financial health of your business, or do you have to sort through piles of convoluted and disorganized data from multiple sources to understand what is happening to your net worth, equity and peace of mind? Are the financial indicators predictive or are you examining historic information that tells you about the past but fails to give you a future oriented roadmap? Do you truly understand what you are tracking and what to do with the information once it is on your radar screen?

Personally, my eyes and interest tend to glaze over and dull when examining stacks of financial information. Somehow all those columns, ratios, balances, and margin lines do not excite me as much as making a sale, motivating an employee, or giving a well thought out, inspiring "state of the company" speech. Being a recovering liberal arts major, I would rather participate in an intimate conversation with another person than pour over statistics that are not linked to a local sports franchise and highlighted in the morning's sports section. If you are like me, and leading a business, you had better quickly get over what you do not like to do, bite the bullet, and educate yourself on sound, fundamental, financial management. Better yet, surround yourself with people who do get their jollies looking at charts, graphs, trends, and are good communicators to boot (that is a rare breed).

If you were stranded on a deserted, tropical island armed with a cell phone, limited minutes available, and could call your business only once a month without being slammed into voicemail hell, what would you want to know that would indicate to you that your doors would remain open the next day? What financial data, in a flash, would reveal to you the macro picture regarding the true current and future financial health of your company? What information would allow you to sleep well that evening in your bamboo hut or motivate you to jump into a dugout canoe, paddle furiously to some appropriate destination to initiate immediate, corrective action?

What would be on your company's flash report? That is your box score. Figure it out and know it well.

You must custom design this snapshot. It must make impeccable, explicit sense to you. It must tell you what you need to know about your business, and not be so generic that it could easily slide into any company, giving any examiner "one shoe fits all" general information. Obviously, some of the areas you will need data on are revenue, profitability, and cash flow. More importantly, you need to monitor the factors and indicators that affect them. You want causes not symptoms. Those are your business's vital internal organs. They keep you alive and you cannot afford to have your monitors suddenly and unexpectedly indicate that your vital signs have flat-lined. We do not want to hear somebody on your staff yell out "clear."

How you measure those ingredients and what individual specific twists you put on them must be restricted to your business and relative to how you personally digest and evaluate information. If you are anal, bring on the spreadsheets and ratios. If visual, how about some color charts and graphs or a power-point presentation? If you like written narratives, then get the information in story form. If you are verbal, then have someone tell you what is going on with your business. Do something that works for you.

Scan all the elements that significantly make your business successful and pinpoint exact areas of importance that you need to closely and periodically scrutinize. Things to consider range from strict, hard line, financial data to company culture issues. You make the choices.

Keep the following in mind when setting up your specific flash report items:

- The items must be predictive, not solely historical.
- The items must be easily understood and obtainable.
- The items must be timely, scheduled, and relevant.
- Keep the items few in number and high in impact.
- Do not lock onto them forever. Your business may change and the information provided no longer reveals to you what you need to know.
- Have others outside your business periodically and objectively review the information.
- Act upon the data as needed.
- That is enough. Now go out to lunch.

Do not fly blind.

Imagine that you are progressing up the ladder in securing your pilot's license and it is now time for the dreaded, up in the sky, instrument-rating test. You and your instructor climb into the cockpit and fasten your seat belts; you in the pilot's seat, an experienced teacher in the jump seat with cool, orange-lens sunglasses and leather flight jacket.

The take-off is smooth. You bank left away from the airport, level out at 10,000 feet, compass reading due North, ground speed approximately 145 mph, and wait for further instructions. Your instructor, with your cooperation, secures an opaque hood over your head and the panel before you. You are suddenly blind to the horizon and everything else. All of your senses go up a notch or two. You are told to continue to fly the plane relying solely on the instruments on the cockpit panel, under your hood. As you follow the instructions, you discover that all the instruments essential for safely flying the aircraft have been painted over with black paint and you cannot see the dials, gauges, or anything else relative to the instruments. It is pitch black. Sweat pours from your forehead and palms. Your insides begin to churn. Panic sets in as you realize that you could crash and burn if something is not done to immediately correct the situation.

This can happen to you in your business if you do not have current, reliable, and accurate financial information on the company you are piloting. Flying financially blind, at some point, will cause you to bury your enterprise into the ground.

In 15 years, I had only one short-term TEC member crash and burn. I have some accountability for this as I let him join the TEC Group, as an unsophisticated business executive, leading a company that he had allowed to become chronically ill. I did not perform proper due diligence but we all learned from the experience. Sometimes having a picture of what not to do is as valuable as witnessing the right way.

Ralph was in his sixth year of owning and leading his own distribution business. He was generating mid-seven figure revenues. Having survived that long, I assumed his financial house was in good order. He background was sales and marketing. He knew how to move merchandize from manufacturer, to warehouse, to retail outlets. His customers liked him, as he was handsome, charismatic, and enjoyable to be around. Being seemingly open, a good communicator and easy to be with, I immediately felt a kinship with him.

Welcoming him into the TEC Group, I bypassed the interviewing procedure that had proven valuable to me and other prospective members in the past. I overlooked trusting the process. Owning his own company was always Ralph's dream, and barely into his forties, he had accomplished just that and was now going to sit monthly at the conference table with seasoned and successful CEOs. Welcome to the big leagues.

In preparation for his first TEC meeting, I requested that he share with the group what they would need to know in order to assist him further on down the road when issues came to the forefront. He thought that was a good idea but would like to take it one step further by presenting an issue to the group in his first meeting. He would like some immediate assistance on one particular subject. I thought that would be fine to jump-start him into what we did every month.

We discussed the issue and the process and both agreed that having the group appraise his financials would be an important bit of information in helping resolve his "temporary" cash flow problems. I asked to review his income and cash flow statements and to study his balance sheet before the group did. He explained that the October statements were not available as his bookkeeper was on vacation, but he would have them in time to show the members at the November meeting to support his issue. A red flag was going up the pole and I was in denial.

Fast forward to the November TEC meeting. For about 30 minutes, the group listened to a narrative from Ralph about his cash flow woes, and then spent considerable time reviewing a stack of copied documents that he tried to pass on as his current balance sheet and income statement. The data was disorganized, outdated, coming from multiple sources and software programs, sprinkled with a multitude of errors, and missing vital information. Ralph appeared shaken and embarrassed. So was I.

Ted went first. "Ralph, you seem like a nice guy and I hate to say this since I just met you, but based upon what you have told and showed us this afternoon your ass is grass and your banker, the government, and your suppliers are the lawnmowers. You are out of business, have been for some time, and you don't seem to get it. How could you let this happen?" The room became quiet. Smiles went south as each member focused on Ralph and perhaps reflected upon their own businesses and how this might happen to them if they did not pay diligent attention to their own finances.

"This is extremely serious and unless you have an angel somewhere you're basically toast." Harsh words to a new member from a veteran, financially savvy, successful company president. Ted was appalled. His voice stern, his body language closed and resigned. I knew I would hear from Ted after the meeting. Our new member was not an appropriate fit. Ted did not intend to be cruel or crude but he wanted to get this relatively new CEO's attention and to cut to the chase. Besides, Ralph was wasting our time as the situation was beyond repair and we had other member's issues to work on that afternoon.

A chagrined Ralph shared with us that he had not had current financial information on his business for over 10 months. He was too busy and caught up in performing his role of saving existing accounts and securing new business for the organization. Plus, he was not comfortable with finances. He subordinated all that fiscal activity to the incapable hands of his part-time bookkeeper. He was now paying big time for that decision. What he knew was that money was tight and everything would work itself out in the end. After all, it always had in the past.

When he finally managed to patch something together for the meeting he did not understand what the numbers were telling him. As a group, we did understand, but with the resources he had available, it was too late to do anything constructive about it. Ralph had used the group, as a last gasp effort to save his business while facing what he intuitively knew was the inevitable truth. He was finished and that was a difficult pill to for him to swallow. It would for anyone.

The group gave Ralph good advice on how to ethically and morally shut the business down, deal with vendors, the bank, and squeeze what he could out of what he had available to him. We were all sorry that this was happening to a seemingly well-intended man. Two months later, the bank called the loan, suppliers cut him off, he sold or returned his inventory for discounted dollars, threw the business into bankruptcy, and went to work for a competitor selling product, and began once again to sleep through the night. It was a deep hole to crawl out of but at the very least, he had a monthly paycheck coming.

My most successful clients and TEC members demand that all of their financial reports be given to them on time and when they want them. They insist that the reports be accurate and inform them in customized detail relative to what they want and need to know. They make certain that the form in which the information reaches them is understandable by them and consistent with how they process information. When they recognize warning signals that they are headed in the wrong direction, they take immediate, corrective action. Periodically, they have outsiders review their statements for accuracy and objective interpretation. Most spend quality time with those providing them the reports. They get to know their financial people better than anyone else in their organization.

If you are not receiving your reports, in the above-mentioned fashion, then raise hell and get everyone back on your track. It is your net worth that you are protecting and expanding. You deserve every opportunity to increase it. Howard Hughes got it right when he said, "I'm not a paranoid deranged millionaire. Goddamit, I'm a billionaire." If conditions do not improve then make the necessary personnel changes and find someone who understands what you want and is committed to delivering the goods to you exactly the way you want them.

Insist upon financial literacy.

During the open book management craze, I witnessed many well intended business leaders make a significant effort at sharing financial information with their employees. They had digested just enough information and process regarding this management flavor-of-the-month to be armed and dangerous. It usually took on this form. The CEO and the in-house financial guru, ranging from a bookkeeper, controller to CFO, would decide upon basic financial information to share with the employees. It seemed like a good idea to let the employees know where the company stood from a fiscal standpoint so that they could play a part in improving the numbers that were being made visible. It was truly a watered down version of the total program of open book management and deserved more attention to make the process more effective.

Pinned up on the "sue the company for free bulletin board" alongside of all the human resources compliance notices, government and union threats went the designated numbers. Impressive, informative, but what the hell do they all mean? The casual observer immediately noticed that sales for fiscal year 2003 were $20 million and net profit was 10%. It did not take much of a self-acclaimed, financial genius to conclude that the owner had obviously pocketed $2 million and the damn tightwad won't even match my 401K at any significant percentage or buy the sales staff those new cell phones that they have been complaining about not having.

If you are going to make your numbers visible to your employee base, you must accompany the information with continuous, financial literacy training. My assumption is that in most companies few people truly understand an income or cash flow statement, let alone your balance sheet. One other startling assumption is that most of them do not really care to learn. Your winners do, so hang in there. Break it down to connect the employee's task with the numbers you are attempting to impact so that they do get it. Demonstrate to them what areas of the various financial statements they can influence by doing their tasks more efficiently, by buying more intelligently, by managing what is important rather than what is familiar or comfortable, by doing the right things that they have control over. Pay attention to the insight of comedian and actor Woody Allen, who said, "Organized crime in America takes in over $40 billion a year, and spends very little on office supplies." What are you allowing your organization to spend too much on?

Make available to your employees opportunities for enrolling into in-house or on-campus financial training seminars. Internally, your financial guru can spotlight the areas on the financials that make sense to the individual employees and address what they do at work that would significantly affect the statements. Banks provide classes on financial management. Local colleges offer evening financial curriculum at low tuition rates. There are abundant resources available if you have someone investigate and select. Because you are a business and your scorecard is financial, you had better educate your employees on the business of being in business. Granted not all employees will be interested, but why punish the rest who are by not offering and encouraging participation? Remember "keepers" want to learn and expand their business acumen.

Review: To be a successful and effective leader of a small to midsize business you must:

1. **Make money and get everyone's attention.**
2. **Pound your financial stakes in terra firma.**
3. **Create your box score.**
4. **Do not fly blind.**
5. **Insist upon financial literacy.**

Robust actions to take:

1. Identify your financial stakes for your organization.

2. Determine the financial indicators in your corporate box score.

3. Select the financial reports that you need. When do you need them? In what form? Who should provide them to you?

4. State how you are going to communicate your financials to your organization. Identify what is going to be communicated.

Chapter Seven

STRATEGY SEVEN: SET YOUR PLAN IN MOTION WITH ONE HAND ON THE REVERSE GEAR

When the horse is dead, get off.

—Anonymous

Keep constant vigilance.

Anonymous is right. However, make sure that your chosen strategic mount has actually rolled over and taken its last gasp breath before you discard it to the local glue factory. As "Honest Abe" said, "It is not best to swap horses while crossing the river." You can go deep underwater doing that. Leaders should undertake new business strategies only after their current choice has reached its logical and final conclusion.

Pay attention to what is or is not working. Do not be so involved in working in your business that you forget to work on the business from the perspective of an external objective observer rather than an internal passionate participant.

Remember that the last nine words of any dying business is, "This is the way we have always done it." You must constantly examine, explore, and test what, how, and why you are doing what you are doing. Whether it hints, whispers or shouts back at you that something is not working, make intentional, well considered, and appropriate changes. While the economy tends to slow down, speed up, and experiences spurts and sputters, the velocity of change continues to accelerate aggressively forward at a rate never before encountered. Jack, when at General Electric, suggested, "When the external rate of change exceeds the internal rate of change, the end is near." You cannot assume that what worked yesterday will work today, tomorrow or ever again. Constant and vigilant calibration is necessary in today's global and instantly connected business environment.

It is impossible to change a tire tearing down the highway at 80 miles per hour in your turbo-charged convertible with the wind in your face and bugs stuck between your teeth. If your wheels are deflating or gone completely flat, you should pull over and put on the new tire or pump fresh air in the old one. What is your air gauge telling you?

The same applies when at the wheel of a stalled or out-of-control business headed toward an unanticipated ditch, or not firing on all cylinders. Put on the breaks, slow down and come to a controlled stop. Deliberately, carefully, with all your senses on full alert, select the reverse gear and ease the business back to disengage and free yourself from the collision. Step out of whatever you are driving and position yourself so that you can view the situation from another perspective and intelligently explore what caused the wreck rather than settling for a quick snapshot of the accident scene. It would be inappropriate, foolish, and irresponsible to stubbornly roar on, engine racing, wind again in your face, white knuckling forward, when the evidence presenting itself through the windshield, in full living color, suggests an immediate pit stop. You are not an all-terrain vehicle. Be resilient not persistent.

In business, unlike with people, the past is not always the best predictor of future, guaranteed success. Remember Xerox, IBM, Eastman Kodak, and Polaroid. These international behemoths hit the skids hard in the 1990s as they ignored penetration into their traditional markets by competitors that were not the usual suspects. The new players were simply discounted and dismissed. Learn this lesson. Do not become arrogant and fall in love with what you believe is your inherent right to be number one with your customers and that your well-established, traditional competitive edge will last forever. If your focus is on keeping your edge razor-sharp, using that familiar back and forth stroke on the same timeworn leather strap, it just may turn against you one day and slit your self-serving throat. Sir Winston Churchill said, "However beautiful the strategy, you should occasionally look at the results." That is a good and appropriate idea.

Hire and train strategic thinkers.

Strategically moving your business forward is an all-consuming and encompassing task. You cannot do this alone. You need to team internally with what Rudyard Kipling identifies as his "six honest men."

> I keep six honest men
> (they taught me all I knew);
> Their names are What and Why and When
> And How and Where and Who.
> —From The Elephant's Child
> By Rudyard Kipling

Strategic thinking and deliberate intelligent application primarily focuses on one of the six honest men, Mr. **"How."** When you think of strategy, think of "How am I going to accomplish something? How am I going to come to market? How am I going to compete with the behemoths? How is this organization going to become unstuck, etc.?" In the strategy lies the answer. Eventually, all the other "honest men," where, what, why, when, and who, join in and play their cameo roles in the creation and implementation of the plan.

Do you have among your employees a Mr. **"Who"** that can intelligently, consistently, and effectively, team with you to determine how you are going to strategically accelerate your organization toward your vision? Experience unfortunately suggests, "probably not." You do not have an internal human inventory of well-educated, perceptive, experienced MBAs at your disposal to strategize your next move.

Mr. **"When"** enters the scene as the immediate response to identified problems or the initiating of appropriate changes. Do not procrastinate. Be decisive. He is action oriented and very impatient.

Mr. **"What"** is simply the goals and the vision that you are driving the organization toward.

Mr. **"Why"** is the justification of whatever you are implementing, the intention motivating you to accomplish something. It needs to be appropriate and focused on doing the right things.

Mr. **"Where"** is whatever market you are attempting to penetrate. It may be geographical or vertical but it needs to be clearly defined.

Small to midsize companies usually create and organize themselves in a "silo" structure relative to the management level on the organization chart. You have a definitive silo where the beans are counted, another silo is for sales and marketing management, one exists for operations to thrash around in, and on down the horizontal and vertical lines you classify specific functions and hire captains to perform admirably within their defined boundaries and job descriptions. Seldom do the captains assist you in strategizing, at the same level that the MBAs do at Fortune 500 companies. Seldom do they possess the perspective of an owner, CEO, or are able to look down at the business from a 30,000-foot elevation. You cannot find fault with that because you did not hire them to fulfill that strategic role. They are mired in their own fishbowl swimming about in their own familiar water doing what is comfortable, known, and predictable. You need to change this.

Not to worry. My most forward thinking, successful TEC members, and corporate clients partially overcame this situation by executing the following strategy regarding their direct reports that they stuffed in their silos. Classify your managers into the following three categories.

Category one: the stars: Evaluate your roster and select those that have demonstrated the most consistent ability in assisting you to move the organization strategically forward. Single them out and inform them of their role. They are allowed to sit with you at the strategic planning conference table and suggest appropriate strategic input. Provide them leadership and strategic training, and challenge them to reach their "Peter Principle," then push them to go one rung higher, then one more. Teach them what you know that propelled you to the chair that you are sitting in.

As a leader, you are obligated to pay special attention and continue to further develop your stars. Remember to spend 80% of your time developing your top 20%. If you cannot identify anyone to sit with you, you are probable already upside down in the ditch, wheels spinning, or approaching terminal burnout because you are doing it all yourself continually working on the same familiar issues. You might consider selling the business, doing something that you really enjoy, and getting your life back in some semblance of balance.

Category two: the rising stars: For those employees on the organization chart who show promise, untapped potential and keen interest, provide them specific training, mentoring, coaching, role modeling, and the occasional opportunity to participate strategically with you and the chosen stars. Design a professional internal and external development program to accelerate them to stardom. They are your winners-in-waiting.

You may have a future star being blocked in a silo by a category three manager. That does happen. Evaluate the situation and if appropriate terminate that manager. The winners-in-waiting should be given the opportunity to strut their stuff and demonstrate what they are capable of doing. You must choose to pay close attention to this group; they are your future.

Category three: the black holes: For those that historically display limited ability and/or interest and are still patiently standing in line collecting your "company welfare check," have HR escort them to the nearest exit and wish them and their new employer well. They are a drain on your net worth and equity. Are you finally getting the point that what I am relentlessly preaching is the creation and protection of your financial security?

Replace the black hole slackers with those that demonstrate, through past, validated experience, the ability to think strategically and perform a designated function in the organization at an elevated level. You need to recruit and interview for these traits.

Upgrading the talent within the silos at every opportunity

is essential and keeps you in the present and future game that you have chosen to compete in. You had better have solidly in place a proactive talent search and a defined process to quickly evaluate the people who show up at your door.

Define the role of your strategic management team.

The role of a strategic thinking management team and their designated leader is to intelligently strategize and implement the following four activities:

- Continually evaluate the present and future needs of your customers.
- Satisfy those needs profitably.
- Continually monitor your competition.
- Keep your competitive advantage appropriate.

Continually evaluate the present and future needs of your customer.

I intentionally chose "needs" not "wants." If you attempt to provide your customers with all that they want they will pick you clean and you will value-add yourself right out of a once profitable business and wonder, in the name of a completely satisfied customer, what in the world happened. "I thought I was doing things right." Well you were but you should have been doing the right things. You do not have to be everything to all people, at all times, under all conditions. Specialize. Do not be run ragged, or held hostage, by your highest volume and loudest customers. Let other suppliers provide your customers their specialties. Be willing to say "no" and do not always assume that your loudest and highest volume customer has the most credibility.

You need to consistently stick with what you do best and

continue to improve that specific offering. When you completely turnkey your product, you tend to dilute your core competency, send unnecessary dollars down the toilet, and lose sight and grasp of your expertise, unless your core competency is providing your customer a "turnkey" experience.

Occasionally, it is a good idea to actually ask your customer, "Do you value all that we are providing, and is it helping you and your business be successful?" That should be a CEO-to-CEO continual conversation. Become the Chief Sales Officer along with being the CEO. You might be astounded to hear, "This is all very nice, but what we would really like is a lower price per unit and you can keep all the value-added offerings that are increasing your costs that I suspect you are now passing on to me. We simply do not value it as much as you do."

Ask the customer; now that is an interesting concept. Remember the words of comedian Bill Cosby who said, "I don't know the key to success, but the key to failure is trying to please everybody."

The majority of the time small to midsize companies focus on meeting and understanding the present needs of their customers because that provides the river of cash required to keep the doors open. With their nose to the grindstone and attention riveted upon getting the next order shipped, they often lose sight of the future and the opportunity to be at the intersection when a new offering and their customer's unique needs simultaneously engage.

With limited resources, you are still able to collect data that when gathered and analyzed will provide you an educated peek into your customer's future needs. Try the following:

- Always debrief your sales people when they come in from the cold. What did they learn about your customers?

- Make CEO-to-CEO sales calls on your best customers and ask only questions that identify what the customer needs from you to make their business more successful.
- Check out your customer and competitor web sites.
- Attend customer and your industry trade shows.
- Gather all employees who interact with your customers and brainstorm new and innovative ways you can improve customer relationships.
- Subscribe to and read your market's publications looking for trends, etc.
- Create focus group with your best customers and ask them what they need from you.
- Warehouse all this information, and with objective external input, analyze what the data is telling you.

All of these activities are minimal cost items providing low-hanging fruit for you to pick, digest, and make appropriate choices regarding your customer's needs and direction. Do something. Do not be squandering your time hanging out on some familiar street corner waiting for your market to sucker punch you squarely on your nose because you are too busy, looking one inch in front of you, doing what you have always done in the manner that you have always done it. Does this make sense?

One does not have to go back too far in history to see how quickly markets can change, needs are identified, strategies evolved, and new and existing customers are rapidly satisfied by "unusual suspects."

In the past, books were primarily purchased through local corner bookstores. The owners and operators of those businesses provided somewhat limited inventories, priced their products competitively, and developed a loyal customer base. The businesses were doing fine. They were not setting the world on fire, but they were producing moderate profits and satisfying the needs of a defined market of owners and book buyers. The owners and operators also had unconsciously and collectively reached over and pressed the snooze button.

While all this was taking place, some seemingly smart people noticed that a large population of consumers was wandering about in huge cavernous concrete boxes, with massive parking lots, purchasing all types of merchandize in mammoth volumes. Boxes of Tylenol were seen roped onto the tops of automobiles. A one-year supply of toilet paper was being sandwiched between hyperactive, suburban preschoolers in the back seats of Ford Expeditions.

Why not books? Enter Borders, Barnes and Noble, and others. Instantly, some of the corner bookstores toppled off the radar screen. The behemoths strutted around with brand-new bricks and mortar, unlimited inventory, Starbucks coffee, low everyday pricing, anchor tenant status, elaborate branding strategies and bulging budgets. They were feeling good about penetrating this market with a unique delivery channel that met the needs of a growing, interested, and consuming market. They had successfully implemented their Wall Street business plan.

Some other intelligent folks noticed that there was a large and growing population of consumers that were comfortable and familiar with buying a variety of merchandize online. Why not books? Enter Amazon and diminishing market share for the big boxes and corner bookstores. Amazon went global the instant they went into business. That was hardly fair, traditional, or expected.

Spending enormous sums of investor money on marketing a limited number of products, the brain trust at Amazon concluded that if they continued on that path it would lead to one of those nasty train wrecks. Resetting their strategy, they noticed that they had a gazillion credit card numbers, e-mail addresses, and a process that was proven successful. Not a bad formula for mass merchandizing a variety of products and positioning themselves as an online shopping mall. Things change and you need to change with them at the same or at an accelerated rate.

All of this happened very quickly and with little advance warning. As you read this book brilliant people, with deep pockets, are spending time, energy, and money figuring out the next opportunity to satisfy an emerging, voracious market. You may be the bulls-eye in their laser-focused, high-powered arsenal.

You are now competing in a rapidly changing and evolving world. Your advantage is your nimbleness and your ability to act upon information quickly. You have the ability to walk outside your office and shout at full volume to your stars "left," and the organization can and perhaps will move in that direction without passing through hoops of meetings, board approval and volumes of data.

Keep your eye on the future and do your best to figure out how you are going to profitably participate in satisfying the present and future needs of the customers you choose to do business with.

Satisfy those needs profitably.

Unless you are burning an endless supply of investor money, as a small to midsize business, your financial well is only so deep and can quickly go dry if you are not paying attention to your numbers. You cannot afford to be fiscally promiscuous by ignoring your own monetary needs in an effort to satisfy a demanding customer who will drop you like a hot, glowing coal the moment a competitor comes in with a lower price per unit. Yes, you can build firewalls around the account by extraordinary service, on-time deliveries, face-to-face interaction, and all the rest. However, the fact remains that all customers are temporary due to the significance of the box score and the inevitable and eventual fate of all products, at some point in their life cycle, being coldly tossed into the commodity bin where price rules. Ultimately the numbers drive nearly all business decisions and relationships.

There will be times when you are forced to sacrifice profits in the name of growing your business and investing for the future, but be prudent. I had a TEC member in the high-end wood frame window business. Vern had successfully and with great care shepherded a family business into its third generation. Statistically that is quite an accomplishment. While at the helm he grew the top and bottom line, and developed a well-earned reputation with local builders and distributors as a quality, dependable, branded supplier. In an effort to expand his business and diversify his offering, he diluted his traditional wood frame window business by venturing into manufacturing vinyl-framed windows. At the time, it seemed like a good, intelligent strategy. The product was appealing to builders because of its shelf life and cost. He invested considerable cash in new state-of-the-art manufacturing equipment, hired additional employees to produce the product, and diverted his and the company's focus to recruiting and securing fresh customers.

Vern went fishing, set the hook, and landed a promising new customer who was a demanding, national chain, big box, home improvement retail store. This was virgin and exciting territory. In order to meet the behemoth's needs of high volume, low price, and delivery to multiple locations, he found himself compromising his business model and placing in harm's way the consistent profits and focus that his traditional products had historically provided. He felt like a puppet on a string dancing to the unpredictable and unfamiliar whims, needs, and wants of an uncaring giant. It was an impending train wreck in the making.

After considerable anguish, Vern pulled the plug on his newest, most prestigious customer and began to pay more attention to manufacturing his core products and selling them to established and familiar customers.

At times you need to muster up the courage and fire a customer because they are not always right and especially not always right for you. Vern continues to produce the vinyl window frames but now sells them to customers who will negotiate and agree to a fair and equitable price at a fair and equitable margin. He did the right thing.

Monitor your competition.

If you are selling into a viable market and knocking down sizable profits, you are going to draw attention because of your success, and someone is going to notice. Hello competition. Like bears to a honey jar, you will be discovered and attempts will be made by others to penetrate your playpen and take away market share and margins. Pay attention to who these folks are and how these players come to your market. The bullet that can kill you is usually the one you do not see being fired from a sniper's nest.

Like the Godfather said, "Keep your friends close but keep your enemies closer." Get your antennas telescoped skyward, turn your radar on to sweep the horizon, calibrate your GPS system, and analyze the data. It is much easier and less costly to emulate rather than initiate. It is much more effective to strategize defensive and offensive maneuvers once you know who the enemy is, where they are, and how they operate.

Sleuth around and gather as much "intel" as you are able to. Turn your marketing people into Chief Intelligence Officers. Copy what works for your competition and put your own spin on their process that fits with how you like to do business. I do not believe in the old adage that, "If we just keep focused on what we do well, to heck with the others guys, everything will work out." You are not the only leader who has found success and can implement innovative ideas.

Keep your competitive advantage appropriate.

Bruce Henderson, founder of the Boston Consulting Group, shares his thoughts on competitive advantage in a 1989 Harvard Business Review article: Henderson writes; "Strategy ... a deliberate search for a plan of action that will develop a business's competitive advantage and compound it. For any company the search is an interactive process that begins with recognition of where you are and what you have now. Your most dangerous competitors are those that are most like you. The differences between you and your competitors are the basis of your advantage. If you are in business and self-supporting, you already have some kind of competitive advantage no matter how small or subtle. Otherwise, you would have gradually lost customers faster than you gained them. The objective is to enlarge the scope of the advantage which can only happen at someone else's expense."

And I say, "Amen, and do not fall in love with it."

Ben Franklin proposed that, "It is hard for an empty bag to stand upright. Your current competitive advantage had better have some relevance and substance to it or you are history. No amount of money, brilliant execution, advertising, employee perks or anything else is going to support or rescue an inappropriate and weak business proposition.

Keep this advantage singular so you can keep it sharp, and focus your resources on what is vital and essential to your success. Make it highly visible to the organization so it is thoroughly understood and available to consciously refine. Your competitive advantage should inspire you and the organization to exceed all previous expectations. It should motivate customers to continue to do business with you. It should attract prospects to join you on your journey. It should be a beacon for talented people to climb on board. It should be a rail to ride to your explicit vision. The advantage should leapfrog you over competitors and enable the business to leap tall buildings with a single bound instead of incrementally grinding it out. A compelling competitive advantage should accelerate your company to being a market leader and viewed by the world you do business in as the best and the only enterprise that they should do business with.

Review: To be a successful and effective leader of a small to midsize business you must:

1. **Keep constant vigilance.**
2. **Hire and train strategic thinkers.**
3. **Satisfy those needs profitably.**
4. **Monitor your competition.**
5. **Keep your competitive advantage appropriate.**

Robust actions to take:

1. **What** are you trying to accomplish in your business?

2. **Why** are you trying to accomplish this?

3. **When** do you want this completed?

4. **How** are you going to do this?

5. **Where** is this all going to take place?

6. **Who** is going to do the work?

7. **Who** is your most feared competitor?

8. **What** is your competitive edge that defines why you are the first choice of customers?

Ole Carlson, author, corporate trainer, strategic planning consultant, and keynote speaker, has spoken to CEO audiences in the United States, Canada, the United Kingdom, Mexico, and Australia, on leadership, personal growth, and strategic planning. He has been a lead trainer for various transformational seminars, serves as CEO coach, group facilitator, and corporate trainer for TEC International, was recognized as TEC Australia's 1999 International Speaker of the Year, TEC Wisconsin's 2001 "Best of the Best," and in 2002, one of TEC International's all-time top 35 speakers.

A graduate of the University of Washington, Ole currently resides in La Quinta, California with his wife, Sue Ann.

9 781413 444346